CREATIVE DESIGN

DRIED & PRESSED FLOWERS

CREATIVE DESIGN

DRIED & PRESSED FLOWERS

Mary Lawrence • Sarah Waterkeyn

GALLERY BOOKS
An Imprint of W. H. Smith Publishers Inc.
112 Madison Avenue
New York City 10016

©Salamander Books Ltd. 1989
52 Bedford Row,
London WC1R 4LR,
United Kingdom.

ISBN 0-8317-2461-7

This edition published in 1989 by Gallery Books,
an imprint of W.H. Smith Publishers, Inc.,
112 Madison Avenue, New York 10016.

Gallery Books are available for bulk purchase for sales
promotion and premium use. For details write or telephone
the Manager of Special Sales, W.H. Smith Publishers, Inc.,
112 Madison Avenue, New York, New York 10016. (212) 532-6600.

CREDITS

Dried flower designs by: Sarah Waterkeyn and John Lewis

Pressed flower designs by: Mary Lawrence

Editor-in-chief: Jilly Glassborow

Editor: Coral Walker

Designer: Kathy Gummer

Photographer: Steve Tanner

Typeset by: The Old Mill, London

Color separation by: Fotographics Ltd, London — Hong Kong

Printed in Italy

CONTENTS

INTRODUCTION

Today, dried and pressed flower arranging is a popular and relaxing pastime, associated with designs as packed with colour and variety as any fresh flower arrangement. And the displays are there to be enjoyed for years rather than merely days.

Divided into two sections, this colourful book will guide you through all stages of both hobbies, from growing and buying the flowers to creating the finished design. Each section opens with a detailed introduction to the various techniques involved, such as how to dry the flowers and wire them into bunches, or make a press and fix the flowers in an arrangement, and there are two beautiful colour plates illustrating some of the more commonly-used plants. The designs themselves range from garlands, wreaths, mobiles, pomanders and centrepieces — all made using dried flowers — to pictures, greeting cards, paperweights and many more novelty ideas made with a beautiful array of pressed flowers.

Except in those cases where the Latin name is more often used, most plants have been given their common names (with alternative US names appearing in brackets). But as common names can vary so much, the scientific names of plants have also been given on page 94.

DRIED FLOWERS

In recent years the popularity of dried flowers has soared as the variety and availability of plant material has increased one-hundred-fold. Whereas twenty years ago choice was restricted to a few common flowers and grasses, such as pampas grass, helichrysum (strawflowers or everlasting) and limonium (statice and sea lavender), today a host of specialist shops are bursting with exciting and colourful flowers from all over the world — plants such as proteas, dryandras and leucodendrons.

BUYING DRIED FLOWERS

When buying dried flowers, the wide range of plants now available may at first seem confusing. The beginner might be well advised to start by purchasing mixed bunches which can usually be bought in large department stores, gift shops and some fresh flower shops. But for real variety, it is best to buy individual bunches from a specialist shop. Often, only three or four varieties are all you need to create a colourful and imaginative display.

Decide what colours you want first, either choosing complementary colours such as yellows and oranges, reds and pinks, blues and purples or picking strikingly contrasting colours — yellows and purples, reds and blues, pinks and oranges. Think also about tonal contrast in your arrangement: white and yellow add welcome highlights to dark displays; dark browns or greens give depth to bright arrangements.

Shape and texture are also very important when planning a display; unusual shapes and contrasting textures add interest and can prevent an arrangement from looking uninspired. The illustration below shows some of the unusual things you can add to your designs, including nuts, cones, fungi, twigs, spices and coral. Ribbons and fabric can also add colour and interest. So when gathering materials for your arrangements, try looking further than your local florist.

GROWING YOUR OWN

Growing your own flowers is by far the cheapest way of pursuing this hobby and has the advantage of providing you with colour in the garden as well as inside the home. Plants should be picked on a dry day just before the flowers are fully open, and preferably in the middle of the day when the sap is rising. If the flowers you pick are wet from rain or dew, before you preserve them, gently shake them and leave the stems standing in some shallow water until the petals are dry.

One of the easiest methods of drying flowers is to hang them upside down in a warm, dark, airy place; this helps to preserve the flowers' natural colour. Not all plants are suitable for drying this way though — others are better preserved using desiccants or glycerine. Drying methods are discussed in more detail opposite.

To avoid leaving large bare patches in your garden after you have gathered the flowers, intersperse the flowers amongst other plants when planting so that their loss is not so noticeable later on. Suitable plants to grow for drying include everlastings such as helichrysum, helipterum, xeranthemum and eryngium (sea holly), plus heather, limonium, larkspur, golden rod, yarrow, lavender, lady's mantle, allium and poppy. Dried roses are beautiful, but multi-petalled varieties are more suitable for preserving than single-petalled ones.

A wide range of materials can be used to add interest to arrangements. Shown left are: 1) pot-pourri; 2) lotus seedheads; 3) repens rosette; 4) platyspernum cones; 5) Leucodendron plumosum; 6) walnuts; 7) coral; 8) sponge mushroom; 9) lagenaria fruit; 10) gourds; 11) artificial berries; 12) willow branch; 13) tallscreen; 14) lomius; 15) cinnamon sticks; 16) Spanish root; 17) cones.

Flowers such as statice, larkspur and pearl achillea can be air dried. Hang them in small bunches, binding the stems first with rubber (elastic) bands.

Also consider growing grasses, ferns and bracken for contrast in your arrangements. Foliage is also important: beech, holly, ivy, bay, hornbeam and lime (linden) are all good for preserving.

If you don't have a garden, pot plants can be a source of material. And keep an eye open on country walks; gather cones, bark, nuts and interestingly shaped twigs from woodlands; wild flowers from meadows, hedgerows and roadsides. Try experimenting with as many plants as you can to see if they are suitable for drying.

DRYING METHODS

There are a number of different ways of drying flowers and foliage and on page 94 you will find a table listing various plants and their methods of preservation. One of the easiest methods is air drying. A number of flowers (particularly the everlastings) can simply be left hanging upside down to dry in a warm, dark, airy place such as an airing cupboard, attic, loft or garage. It is important that the flowers are not put in direct sunlight as this will cause their colours to fade. Bind the flowers together into bunches before hanging them. Rubber bands are best for this purpose as the stems will shrink as they dry. Alternatively, use raffia, pipe cleaners or gardeners' string, being sure to tighten it around the stems regularly.

Suspend the flowers from a pole or some rope and leave them till they are dry and crisp to the touch. Make sure that the stems are completely dry, particularly at the top, otherwise the heads will soon droop. The drying time varies according to the conditions and type of plant, but it usually takes from one to four weeks.

Some plants, such as sea lavender and pampas grass, dry best standing upright in a jam jar or vase. Sand can be used to weight the jar and support the stems. Other plants should be placed in shallow water — about 5cm (2in) deep — to dry. Hydrangea and gypsophila dry best this way. Most grasses, fungi and twigs should be dried flat on an absorbent surface such as cardboard or newspaper. Leaves dried this way tend to shrivel but do retain their natural colour. To prevent the seeds falling off grasses and cereals, and to give added strength to their stems, spray the plants with hair spray before, or even after, drying.

DESICCANTS

Desiccants — or drying agents — draw moisture from the plants and help to preserve the natural colours and form of flowers. One of the simplest to use — though not the cheapest — is silica gel, which can be bought from most hardware stores. It usually comes in the form of white crystals which should be ground down to a finer grade before using. (Blue indicator crystals are also available — these turn pink when they have absorbed water.) Put a layer of crystals into the base of an airtight container and place several wired flowerheads on top. Using a spoon, carefully cover the flowers with more of the desiccant, making sure that the crystals fall between the petals but do not misshape them. When the flowers are fully covered close the container and leave for a couple of days.

Borax is less expensive than silica gel, though it takes longer to work — at least ten days. Ideally it should be mixed with dry silver sand: three parts borax to two parts sand. Cover the flowers as with the silica gel.

GLYCERINE

A mixture of one part glycerine to two parts warm water is ideal for preserving the shape and suppleness of foliage. Either fully submerge the leaves in the solution (singly or in small sprays) or stand the stems of larger sprays in about 8-10cm (3-4in) of mixture. Cut the stems at a sharp angle and hammer the ends of woody stems to aid absorption. Gradually the glycerine will replace the water in the leaves. Submerged leaves take about two days, whereas plants left standing in the mixture take up to four weeks to dry; start checking after the first week.

Foliage, such as copper beech, can be preserved in a mixture of glycerine and water. This method stops the leaves from becoming brittle and misshapen.

Silica gel is used to preserve the shape and colour of roses. Carefully cover the flower with finely-ground crystals, being sure not to crush the petals.

The picture below shows a range of equipment used in dried flower arranging. Certain items may only be required occasionally, as the need arises — wreath wrap for example is only used when making moss wreaths and garlands — whereas other items are considered essential; no flower arranger could cope for long without a strong pair of florists' scissors, a sharp knife, some wire and blocks of florists' foam.

THE MECHANICS

The various items used to support the flowers in an arrangement are known as the mechanics. Florists' foam is the most popular mechanic. It comes in two forms: one for fresh flower arrangements (designed to absorb and hold water), the other for dried arrangements. The latter, often referred to as dry foam, comes in several shapes and sizes — spheres, blocks and cones — and can easily be cut down to any size or shape to fit a container.

Another much-used mechanic is wire mesh which is particularly good for larger, heavier arrangements. It can either be crumpled into a ball or other shape to fit inside the container or it can be packed with moss to form a more solid base. This latter method is sometimes used for making garlands and wreaths.

SECURING THE MECHANICS

It is sometimes possible to wedge the foam or wire mesh into a container so that it is held firm. But usually you will need to secure it in position. Florists' tape is very useful for attaching foam to the base of a container or, where necessary, for holding two or more pieces of foam together.

Small plastic pinholders are also available for securing foam; they can be stuck down on to the container using fixative and the foam can then be pushed firmly on to the pins. Wire is used for attaching both foam and wire mesh to containers — particularly baskets where the wire can be threaded through the wicker work and the ends twisted together to secure firmly in place.

Plaster of Paris is sometimes used in dried flower arranging to weight top heavy displays or support the mechanics — for example, when making a floral tree (see page 22).

Glue is sometimes used for sticking dry foam on to a container. It is also useful for sticking plant materials together or gluing flowerheads or small posies on to a base, such as a box or a picture frame.

WIRE AND STRING

A variety of wire is used in dried flower arranging. Stub wires are straight lengths of wire that are generally used for supporting single flowerheads or binding together small groups of flowers (see opposite). They are also used for supporting more unusual objects in an arrangement such as nuts, cones and so forth. The wires come in a range of different thicknesses, or gauges. Black reel wire is used for making moss wreaths and garlands, as these require a continuous length of wire (see page 10). You can also buy reels of fine silver florists' wire (sometimes called rose wire) which is used for more delicate work, for example, for binding together posies (see page 39) or, in conjunction with string, for making small garlands (see page 49). Rose wire also comes in short lengths, about 15cm (6in) long. This can be used for binding miniature posies or wiring ribbon bows (see opposite).

The equipment used in dried flower arranging includes: 1) plaster of Paris; 2) dry foam; 3) a sharp knife; 4) strong florists' scissors; 5) wreath wrap; 6) string; 7) florists' tape; 8) fixative; 9) glue; 10) plastic pinholders; 11) fine silver reel (rose) wire 12) black reel wire; 13) 15cm (6in) fine silver (rose) wire; 14, 15, and 16) stub wires; 17) wire mesh.

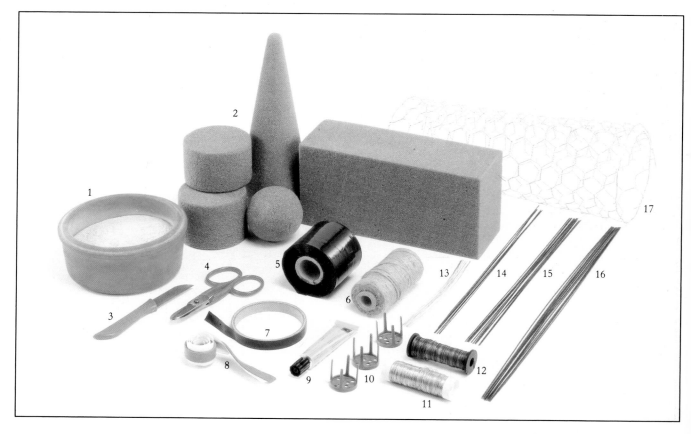

CUTTING IMPLEMENTS

A strong pair of florists' scissors is essential for cutting plants down to size. Some scissors have a special wire-cutting edge; if yours do not, you will also require wire-cutters. Secateurs (pruning shears) are useful for woody stems. A sharp knife is needed for stripping off unwanted leaves and branches from stems, and a second, longer knife is useful for slicing up large blocks of florists' foam.

BASIC TECHNIQUES

Some dried flowers — yarrow and larkspur for example — have strong, firm stems that need no support. Others, such as helichrysums, have weak stems that cannot withstand the weight of the flowerheads. In the latter case, wire can be used to support the flower. Cut a stem down to about 4cm (1½in) and place it against one end of a stub wire. Then bind the length of the stem to the wire using silver reel wire. (If you like, you can then cover the new 'stem' by binding florists' gutta-percha tape around both the plant stem and the stub wire.) This method can also be used for lengthening stems that are too short. For hollow-stemmed plants, such as safflowers and amaranthus, simply push a length of stub wire into the hollow end of the stem.

To increase the impact of colours in a display, flowers are frequently tied into small bunches before they are arranged. To do this, cut down the stems of two or three flowers — weak stems should be cut down to about 4cm (1½in); strong ones can be left longer. Take a length of stub wire and bend back the top 3-4cm (1-1½in) to form a hair-pin shape. Place the pin against the end of the stems, bent end towards the flowerheads. Then, starting about half way down the pin, begin to wind the long end of the wire around both the stems and the short end of the wire. Bind it about three times as shown below, then straighten it so that it forms a 'stem'. Trim the wire to the required length and insert it into the display.

Bows are frequently used to decorate dried flower arrangements. The easiest way to make a perfect bow is to wire it as described right. Other techniques used in dried flower arranging, such as making a garland or wreath, are described on page 10.

To give flowers more impact in a display, wire them into small bunches before arranging them. First bend the end of a stub wire to form a hair-pin shape.

Cut the flower stems short and place them against the pin. Wind the long end of wire round about three times then straighten it to make a 'stem'.

Bows are often used to put the finishing touches to an arrangement. To make this double bow, take a length of satin ribbon about 60cm (2ft) long and make a loop at one end. Form a second loop as shown to make a bow shape. Ensure each time you loop the ribbon that you keep it right side out.

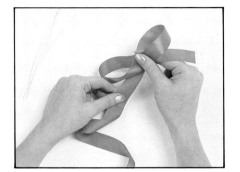

Loop the long tail over the front of the bow to form a third loop, and then to the back to make a fourth loop as shown.

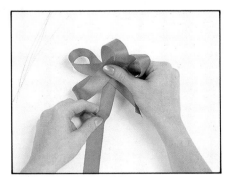

Wrap a length of rose wire round the centre of the bow and secure it by twisting the ends together. Use the ends of the wire to attach the bow to the arrangement. Now simply trim the tails to the required length, cutting them in a V-shape to finish off. This technique can easily be adapted to make a single bow or even a triple or quadruple one.

MAKING A GARLAND

MAKING A WREATH

There are several ways of making a garland; this is but one of them. Another method is shown on page 32. Begin by taking some fresh, damp sphagnum moss. Knead it to get rid of any large lumps, then roll it into a long cylindrical shape. Don't make the roll too thick as the flowers will eventually fatten it up.

To make a wreath such as this you need a wire wreath frame and some dry sphagnum moss. Knead the moss to get rid of any lumps then pack a handful into the frame.

Starting at one end, bind black reel wire tightly round the moss roll, keeping the turns quite close together. Trim off any straggly pieces of moss as you go.

Attach some black reel wire to the frame and, working in an anti-clockwise direction, begin to bind the moss-filled frame, pulling tightly with each turn. Continue to pack and bind the moss into the frame until the whole wreath is complete.

Allow the garland to dry before inserting the flowers. These should be wired in small bunches and inserted at an acute angle into the moss rather than at right angles. A variation on this method, often used for larger garlands, is to roll the moss out on top of a length of wire mesh. You then roll the moss up in the mesh and turn the raw edges of wire under to secure it.

If you like, you can cover the ring with plastic wreath wrap. Attach one end of the wrap to the ring using a wire pin then wind the wrap around the wreath as shown. Wire the flowers into small bunches and insert them into the wreath. Another way to make a wreath is to create a garland as described left: then bend it into a ring and secure the ends with wire.

Helichrysum
(Strawflower or everlasting)

Acroclinium
(also Helipterum — sunray)

Solidago
(Golden rod)

Physalis
(Chinese lantern)

Papaver
(Poppy seedheads)

Rosa
(Rose)

Helichrysum
(South African daisy)

Achillea
(Lonas — a type of yarrow)

Amaranthus
(Love-lies-bleeding)

Lagarus
(Rabbit's or hare's tail grass)

Lunaria
(Honesty)

Xeranthemum

Delphinium
(Larkspur)

Limonium sinuatum
(Statice)

Phalaris
(Reed grass)

Lavandula
(Lavender)

Hydrangea

Hordeum
(Black-eared barley)

Avena fatua
(Wild oats)

Limonium (Goniolimon) tataricum
(Sea lavender)

An old bicycle basket makes the perfect container for this delightfully random display of flowers. First, fill the top of the basket with wire mesh, attaching it to the sides with reel wire threaded through the wicker. Now begin to build up the outline using tall stems of blue larkspur. Fill in the shape using fluffy white gypsophila (baby's breath).

In this attractive design, contrasting colours and textures combine to create a delightful picture. Take a small wicker basket and fill it with wire mesh, attaching the mesh at intervals to the side of the basket with wire. A brightly coloured basket such as this one looks particularly effective. Start to build up the outline of the display using single lengths of blue larkspur.

Complete the outline with wired bunches of sea holly, keeping the shape full and wide. Next, fill in with bunches of large pink helichrysum (strawflower or everlasting). Keep them shorter than the other plants so that they lie lower down in the arrangement.

Finally, pick out the colour of the basket with bunches of bright pink rabbit's or hare's tail grass, scattering them throughout the arrangement and bringing it to life.

Next, position clumps of flowering love-in-a-mist lower down in the arrangement, keeping them well scattered. The focal flowers in the display are pretty pink and yellow acroclinium (sunray). Arrange large clumps of them throughout, keeping the heads well exposed. Finish off with a ring of hydrangea around the rim of the basket.

A combination of lavender and red helichrysum form a delightful surround for this small basket of pot-pourri. Begin by wiring small bunches of lavender — about three to four stems each. Attach a bunch to the rim of the basket by wrapping the wire through the wicker work. Position the next bunch over the stems of the first to cover the wires. Continue round the rim.

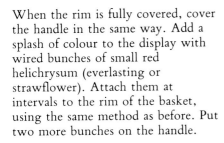

The same basket as the one used opposite but a completely different design — here, netting has been used to create a soft billowing effect. Wire together clumps of red amaranthus (love-lies-bleeding) and insert them at intervals around the rim of the basket. Keep the angles irregular so that some stems are standing up, others hanging down.

When the rim is fully covered, cover the handle in the same way. Add a splash of colour to the display with wired bunches of small red helichrysum (everlasting or strawflower). Attach them at intervals to the rim of the basket, using the same method as before. Put two more bunches on the handle.

Fill in with clumps of blue larkspur and soft pink *Helichrysum casianum*, forming a dense ring of flowers around the basket.

Make a single bow out of deep red ribbon, wiring it together as described on page 9. Attach the bow to the middle of the handle and cover the wire with a strand of lavender; fix this in place using fine silver rose wire. To finish, fill the basket with pot-pourri, choosing a type that complements the colours of the arrangement.

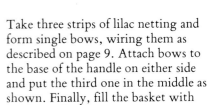

Take three strips of lilac netting and form single bows, wiring them as described on page 9. Attach bows to the base of the handle on either side and put the third one in the middle as shown. Finally, fill the basket with sweet-smelling pot-pourri.

Bring a touch of the country into your living room with this beautiful array of garden flowers. Take a wicker shopping basket and fill the top with wire mesh, attaching the mesh to the sides of the basket with wire. Form a base for the arrangement by packing the mesh with wired bunches of sea lavender.

Wire clumps of love-in-a-mist and insert them into the arrangement so that they stand out above the sea lavender. Then start to fill in with bunches of soft pink larkspur. Try to keep the arrangement slightly parted around the handle so that the latter is not totally obscured. Finish filling in with bunches of lady's mantle, then add several garden roses to complete the picture.

A classic willow pattern vegetable dish serves up an exciting Oriental display of flowers and curling tallscreen. Begin by cutting a block of florists' foam to fit inside the dish. Secure the foam with florists' tape as shown. Prop the lid up against the dish, leaving three quarters of the foam exposed.

Start to build up the general shape of the arrangement using wired clumps of helichrysum (strawflower or everlasting). Then fill in with large bunches of yarrow, covering most of the foam. Keep the shape low and within the outline of the dish.

Add a complete contrast of colour and texture with several stems of tallscreen — their fascinating shape adds interest to any arrangement. Place them at various angles, keeping them taller than the other plants so that they are clearly visible.

Finish off with a few stems of flowering love-in-a-mist, arranging them so that they break out of the general, low-lying outline. The faint hint of blue in these flowers picks up the blue in the dish.

A beautiful old tobacco pot makes a perfect setting for a striking display of brightly coloured flowers. Note how the blue and orange in the china have been picked up by the colours of the flowers. First, cut a block of florists' foam to fit snugly inside the pot.

Using wired bunches of helichrysum (strawflower or everlasting), build up a dome shape to reflect the shape of the pot. Then add clusters of blue-dyed *Leucodendron brunia.* The unusual shape of this plant will always add interest to any arrangement.

Finally, add clumps of bright yellow morrison to fill in any gaps and complete the display.

A giant Minton cup and saucer doubles up as a pot-pourri container. The same effect can easily be created with a normal-sized cup and saucer, using smaller-headed flowers. Make a cylinder out of wire mesh and bend it into a ring large enough to fit around the base of the cup. Knot the ends of the wire together.

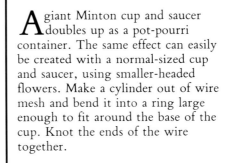

Wire several bunches of deep pink helichrysum (strawflower or everlasting), blue-dyed cluster-flowered sunray and creamy cauliflower. Slot them alternately into the mesh, packing them in tightly to cover the wire but being sure not to obscure the pattern on the side of the cup.

Once the 'garland' has been completed, you can fill the cup with pot-pourri, choosing a mixture that complements the colours of the arrangement.

A beautiful old china jug, bursting with sheaves of oats, makes a striking arrangement for the hallway. Begin by making a garland of flowers to fit round the neck of the jug. Construct the frame of the garland using sphagnum moss and reel wire, following the instructions given in detail on page 10. Leave long tails of wire at either end of the garland.

When the frame is completed, mould a piece of wire mesh into a ball and put it into the jug.

Wrap the moss frame round the neck of the jug and secure it in position by twisting the free ends of the wire together. Select some flowers that co-ordinate with the colours in the jug. Used here are pale blue helichrysum (strawflower or everlasting), blue-dyed achillea and pearl achillea (two types of yarrow).

Wire the flowers into small bunches and insert them into the garland, pushing the wires in at a slight angle rather than at right angles. Arrange the different types alternately, packing them close together to form a thick ring of flowers all the way round the jug.

To complete the display, cut a large amount of oats down to the same height and push them, a bundle at a time, into the wire mesh ball at the base of the jug. Make sure they are packed very tightly and stand straight.

Arrange clumps of sea holly next, sprinkling them throughout. They add an interesting hint of blue to the neutral tones of the arrangement. Now add a dramatic contrast in shape and texture with some large globe thistle heads. Concentrate these around the handle, pushing some deep into the arrangement, and then place a few long stems in the foreground.

This wild arrangement is designed to look like a freshly-gathered basket of flowers and grasses. Use a basket with a low 'lip' at one end and put a ball of wire mesh at the taller end; secure it with wire. Now arrange several large clumps of oats, keeping those at the front long so that they overhang the lip, those further back becoming shorter and more upright.

Now intersperse the oats with wired bunches of love-in-a-mist, maintaining the general shape, with long low-lying stems at the front, shorter upright ones at the back. Follow these with bunches of small poppy seedheads, arranged mainly towards the front of the display so that they appear to be spilling out over the lip. Add a few larger poppy seedheads as well for contrast.

Soften the whole arrangement by adding a few grasses and then finish off by placing several lotus seedheads at the back, using them to cover any exposed wire mesh.

Bring an old frame to life with this attractive arrangement of oats and flowers. Cut four lengths of wire mesh, making them slightly longer than the sides of the frame. Roll them up into tubes about 3cm (1in) in diameter and fix them tightly round the frame, joining them at the corners with wire.

This attractive design illustrates how much a floral arrangement can enhance a plain picture frame — it's easy to do but so very effective. Cut a slice of florists' foam to fit one corner of the frame and tape it in place. Begin to loosely build up the shape using single stems of clubrush.

Wire large clumps of oats and pack them tightly into the wire mesh frame so that the strands become entangled and hold each other together. The oats provide a good base for the other plants and help to keep them in place. Now add wired bunches of yellow anaphalis (pearl everlasting), arranging them at intervals around the frame.

Add a splash of colour throughout the display with bright yellow cressia, allowing some to trail across the frame and picture. Then insert a number of single stems of bottlebrush to add interest and colour.

Position wired bunches of pink *Helichrysum casianum* in amongst the oats, keeping them close to the anaphalis. Finish off with several groups of blue *Leucodendron brunia,* their rich, dark colour adding contrast to the arrangement.

Fill out the display with plenty of bottlebrush foliage. Then add highlights with a few white leaf skeletons such as these peepal leaves.

Finally, make a double bow out of tartan ribbon, following the instructions on page 9. Attach this to the lower portion of the arrangement so that the long tails of the bow trail across the frame. Repeat the whole procedure on the opposite corner, being sure to keep the design well balanced.

Next, make a ring of wire mesh, slightly deeper than the container and wide enough to fit snuggly round it. The ring must be double thickness so you can pack it with dry sphagnum moss. When it is fully packed, neatly bend the raw edges of wire over to close the ring. Now cut several equal lengths of birch twigs and attach them to the moss ring using wire pins — two per twig.

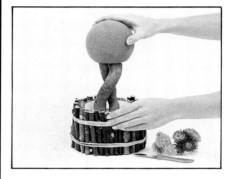

Cover the wire pins by tying long strands of raffia around the ring. Once the plaster has set, place the container inside the wire surround. Take a large sphere of florists' foam and scrape out the centre using a knife. Press the ball on to the wooden 'stem' of the tree, making sure it is held firm. Now wire some small bunches of flowers, leaving at least 3cm (1in) of wire 'tail'.

The flowers used here are orange and yellow helichrysum (strawflower or everlasting), blue larkspur and green amaranthus (love-lies-bleeding). Use the helichrysum first to form the shape, keeping the arrangement spherical. Next add the larkspur and amaranthus, making sure they do not protrude too far out of the arrangement and break up the shape.

This ever-popular form of floral arrangement is not as difficult to achieve as you might think. Begin by selecting a suitable container for the base. Mix up some plaster of Paris with water and fill the container. Quickly insert an interestingly-shaped branch for the stem, holding it in position for a couple of minutes until the plaster begins to set.

Finish off by putting pieces of moss around the base of the tree to hide the plaster of Paris and the wire mesh.

This unusual and imaginative wreath makes a striking decoration to hang on the door during the winter. To create it, you will first need to buy a twig wreath from your local florist. Begin the arrangement by wiring small bunches of oak leaves together. Also take a few pieces of sponge mushroom and push wires through one side.

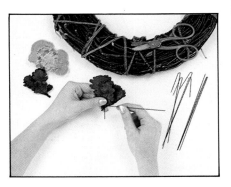

Attach the leaves and fungus to the wreath, forming three groups evenly spaced around the ring. Now wire up some lotus seedheads — wiring the large ones singly and the small ones in groups of two or three. Insert these in amongst the other plants.

Push short lengths of wire as far as they will go through one end of some walnuts. Form small groups of about three to four nuts each by twisting the wires together. Slot the walnuts into the three groups of plants. Next add a few witch hazel twigs, allowing them to break out of the arrangement and cover some bare patches between the groups.

To finish, wire together several bunches of yarrow and slot them into the arrangement, using them to close up the gaps slightly between the three main groups. The yarrow adds necessary colour to the wreath and brings it to life.

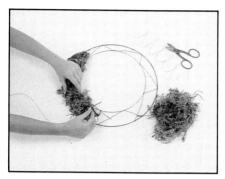

An attractive winter's wreath in muted creams and golds makes a pleasant change from the usual seasonal reds and greens, and gives a different and stylish Christmas decoration. Begin by covering a wreath ring in sphagnum moss, as shown in more detail on page 10.

Co-ordinate a floral display with your curtains or soft furnishings by covering the base in some matching fabric. Take a piece of left-over material and wrap it round a suitable basket. Pack the inside of the basket with wire mesh and hold it in place using strips of wire pushed through both the fabric and the wicker work.

Wire together some clumps of cream sea lavender and virtually cover the entire ring with it. Next, take some purple statice and wire together several bunches.

Intersperse the purple statice evenly amongst the cream coloured flowers which form the base of the garland. Then, place at regular intervals some wired clumps of yarrow and rhodanthe (sunray).

Wire bunches of beige cluster-flowered sunray and bright yellow yarrow and pack them tightly into the wire mesh, forming a dome-shaped outline. Now scatter several wired bunches of reed grass throughout the arrangement.

Finally, gather about 10 to 12 cones and wire them together in a large bunch. With more wire fix the cones to the wreath at the front. Pull a few strands of the flowers between the cones to add contrast. Intersperse a few more cones throughout the wreath as shown to complete the picture. This combination of flowers and cones is remarkably inexpensive, yet the result is quite stunning.

Add large wired bunches of lavender next, keeping the stems long so that the flowers stand out above the other plants. Finish off with groups of South African daisies (a type of helichrysum). These plants have been chosen to match the colours in the fabric so, when you follow this design, alter the range of flowers according to your colour scheme.

This stunning wreath, with its wealth of contrasting colours and materials, makes a beautiful decoration to hang on the door at any time of the year. Begin by making a base (following the instructions given in full on page 10) using a wire frame and some sphagnum moss. Cover the base with green wreath wrap.

Take some colourful fabric and cut it up into rectangles. Now wrap about 8 to 10 small foam spheres in the fabric, gathering the material at the top and securing with wire. Leave long wire 'tails' for attaching the balls to the frame. Position the spheres in groups of two or three at regular intervals around the wreath.

Wire clumps of green amaranthus (love-lies-bleeding) and insert them into the wreath, keeping them generally quite close to the fabric spheres.

Next, wire clumps of white larkspur and intersperse these amongst the amaranthus. These reflect the white in the fabric and add highlights to the arrangement. Wire together several groups of cones and place them standing upright in the arrangement so that they do not get lost among the other plants.

Soften the display by scattering bunches of soft pink rabbit's or hare's tail grass throughout. The seeds tend to moult very easily so be careful when wiring and inserting the grass not to overhandle it.

Pick out the colours in the fabric by dotting clumps of rust coloured nipplewort (or broom bloom) throughout. The dark tones will also add depth to the display.

Finish off with a few colourful satin bows. You can either make double bows (as described on page 9) or single ones as shown here. Insert the bows in amongst the fabric spheres, trailing the tails prettily over the arrangement.

For the celebration of any Scottish event, such as Burns' night (January 26th), create this striking tartan wreath. First you will need to buy a twig ring from a florist. Begin the garland by individually wiring several heads of red rose. Arrange these in three small groups, evenly spaced around the ring.

Next, wire together nine small bunches of anaphalis (pearl everlasting) and push them into the ring so that they surround the roses. Take three lengths of tartan ribbon and make three single bows (following the instructions on page 9).

Take a fourth piece of ribbon, fold it in half and push a piece of wire through the folded end: this will form the long 'tails' of the arrangement. Cut a 'V' shape in the ends of the ribbons to finish them neatly, then wire a bow into each of the three gaps between the flowers. To complete the picture, wire the tartan tails beneath one of the bows.

This beautiful design makes the perfect decoration for Valentine's day. Take some dry, bendy silver birch twigs, trim off all the rough ends and divide them into two equal bundles, about 60cm (24in) long. Join the two bundles at one end with stub wires; and again about 20cm (8in) further along. Now bend either side round to form a heart shape as shown.

Bind the three ends firmly with wire, then wrap wire around four other points on the heart to hold the twigs together. Cover each of the wired areas with red satin or gift wrap ribbon, gluing each strip in place at the back. Wire up a couple of red bows (as described on page 9) and put one on either side of the heart.

Attach a length of wired ribbon to the top of the heart for hanging. To soften the effect, take small clumps of gypsophila (baby's breath) and push them in between the ribbon bands and the twigs. To finish off, mix some more gypsophila with some tiny red spray roses and position them at the base of the heart.

A collection of brilliantly coloured flowers makes a striking display for the sideboard. Begin by moulding some wire mesh into a three-dimensional shape, keeping the base flat and the top end open. Pack the mesh with dry sphagnum moss, then close up the open end. Now insert wired bunches of stirlingia — tall, upright stems at the top, shorter, horizontal ones lower down.

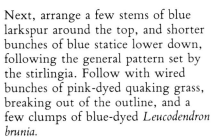

Next, arrange a few stems of blue larkspur around the top, and shorter bunches of blue statice lower down, following the general pattern set by the stirlingia. Follow with wired bunches of pink-dyed quaking grass, breaking out of the outline, and a few clumps of blue-dyed *Leucodendron brunia.*

Once you are happy with the general shape of the arrangement, start to fill in with bunches of large pink helichrysum (strawflower or everlasting). Pack them deep into the display. Add bright yellow highlights next with bunches of cluster-flowered helichrysum.

Finally, wire together a few bunches of rich red roses and scatter them throughout the display. It is important to position the roses last, because this ensures that the heads remain well exposed.

A couple of old wooden spoons form the basis of a pretty arrangement that would brighten up any kitchen. First, wire the spoons together at an angle as shown, winding the wire round the handles several times to secure firmly.

Wire together several small groups of plants, choosing an attractive range of colours. Shown here is yellow quaking grass, white helichrysum (strawflower or everlasting) and dudinea seedheads. Wire the small groups together to form one large bunch and attach this to the spoons so that the blooms sit prettily over the bowls.

Make a large bright double bow out of satin ribbon, following the instructions on page 9, and tie it with a second length of ribbon around the spoons and the posy.

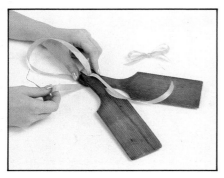

A pair of butter pats makes an unusual setting for this kitchen design. Take a length of ribbon and wire up one end. Thread the ribbon through both holes from the front, leaving a long tail between the pats. Loop the ribbon over the top and thread through from the front again, pulling it tight. Make a second loop in the same way, leaving it long for hanging the display.

Secure the wired end of ribbon at the back with a knot; cut off any excess. Wire a small bow on to the front of the pats. Then attach half a sphere of florists' foam to the ribbon 'tail' using tape. Wire small bunches of blue jasilda and tiny red helichrysum and push them into the ball, packing them tightly together.

Add longer stems of blue larkspur, leaving some pieces trailing down the pats to break up the outline of the ball. Finally, wire up short double loops of ribbon and intersperse them among the flowers, finishing off with a couple of longer strands at the bottom.

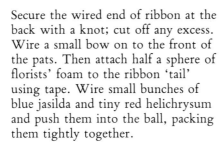

The framework of this seasonal garland is made of cones and walnuts. Wire the cones by wrapping stub wire around the base. For the walnuts, push stub wire through one end as far as it will go. Take a group of cones and nuts and twist the wires together. Add to the base of the group and twist the wires again to secure. Continue in this way until the garland is long enough.

Make a double bow out of gold gift wrap ribbon (following the instructions on page 9) and wire two extra tails on to it. (Just fold a length of ribbon in half for the tails and wire in the middle.) Attach the bow to one end of the garland, then wire a long length of ribbon to the same end. Wrap this through the garland, twisting it round the cones. Leave a long tail at the far end.

To finish, wire together small groups of bright Chinese lanterns and bunches of quaking grass. Intersperse them amongst the cones, entangling the wires to secure them.

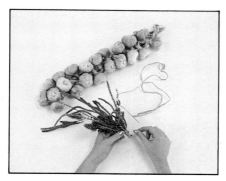

Not as sweet smelling perhaps as some of the other arrangements, but certainly very useful. First make a tied bunch of flowers as follows. Bind a small group of flowers with a length of reel wire. Gradually add more flowers to the bunch, binding them with the same length of wire, until the posy is the desired size.

The flowers used here are rat's tail statice and dryandra. Tie a length of raffia round the end of the posy and finish off with a bow. Wire the posy on to the end of a purchased garland of garlic bulbs. Complete the picture by wiring about five large protea heads and binding them on to the garland in amongst the garlic.

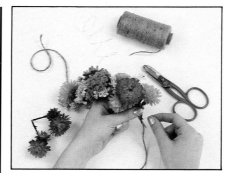

An old cotton spool is transformed by a lively display of bright yellow flowers. Make a garland of flowers as follows. Attach some reel wire to a length of string, about 20cm (8in) from one end. Position a small group of flowers against the join and wrap the wire round the stems to secure. Put another group of flowers over the stems of the first and secure as before.

Continue in this way until the garland is long enough to go round the spool. The flowers used here are brilliant yellow helichrysum (strawflower or everlasting), white larkspur and fluffy golden morrison. Attach the garland to the base of the spool by tying the string round it. Wrap the garland round the spool and secure at the top with the other end of the string.

Don't throw away that old broken flower pot — transform it instead into a stunning autumnal arrangement using black-eared barley and bright yellow helichrysum (strawflower or everlasting). Wedge a piece of florists' foam into the broken pot and secure it with tape. Now build up the shape of the arrangement with the barley, putting the discarded stems to one side.

Place longer stems of barley into the base of the display and generally shorter ones at the top, around the rim. Intersperse the barley with cluster-flowered helichrysum, placing the heads deep in the arrangement. Concentrate the yellow around the rim of the pot to cover up any foam still visible.

Run a line of helichrysum around the broken edge of the pot, pushing the stems into the foam or gluing the heads on if necessary. Finally, take the discarded barley stems and cut off the ends at a sharp angle. Now position them at the back of the display, splaying them out so that they appear to be continuous with the stems at the front.

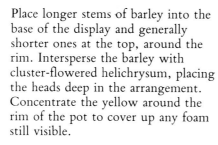

Wood always provides a perfect setting for dried flowers, and an old wooden plane makes a particularly attractive display. Cut a block of florists' foam and wedge it tightly into the hole. Arrange wired clumps of cluster-flowered sunray first, keeping the outline low. Follow with pink *Leucodendron brunia*, allowing it to break out of the shape and dangle low over the sides.

Now add interest and a dash of colour with a few stems of bottlebrush. Put them in singly and keep them short so that their rich colour lies deep within the arrangement.

An attractive wall hanging arrangement puts a redundant towel ring to good use. Begin by slicing a sphere of florists' foam in half and cutting away the centre of one piece so that it fits snugly on top of the ring. Secure the foam with a couple of strips of florists' tape.

Soften the effect with a few clumps of grass interspersed throughout. To finish, add contrasting texture with three or four heads of *Leucodendron plumosum* set deep into the display.

Form the outline of the arrangement with 'blue leaf' foliage. Balance the general shape with that of the ring but create a spiky effect. Fill in with three or so long-eared pods, packed tightly into the foam, and several clumps of beige cluster-flowered sunray. Concentrate the latter in the centre of the arrangement.

Finish off with large bold clumps of yellow helichrysum (strawflower or everlasting) to brighten up the arrangement and blend with the rich tones of the brass ring.

With its soft muted tones and shiny satin ribbons this pretty swag will add a touch of romance to your bedroom. You will need a length of muslin, some satin ribbon and a selection of plants — used here are pink rhodanthe (sunray or Swan River everlasting), pink wheat, oak leaves and leaf skeletons. Begin by wiring the plants into large clumps, leaving long 'tails' of wire.

Cut a strip of muslin about 15cm (6in) wide and 100cm (40in) long. Beginning at one end, gather some of the material into a bunch and secure it by wiring on a bunch of rhodanthe. Repéat the process at regular intervals along the length of the fabric, gathering the muslin into soft folds each time.

To add contrast and depth to the arrangement add clumps of rusty brown oak leaves and whispy leaf skeletons to the rhodanthe. Then attach the pink wheat, arranging it amongst the folds of material.

Make up several double bows using the method described on page 9 and wire them on to the groups of flowers. Use the bows to conceal any wire still showing. Add a couple of long trailing strands of ribbon for the finishing touch. Drape the swag across the end of your bed or around a large mirror.

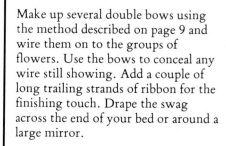

This little collection of hanging baskets would be a pretty addition to a bedroom or bathroom. Take three small straw baskets and place a piece of dry florists' foam inside each one. Take several clumps of wired pink miniature sunray and insert them in the first basket, keeping the flowers close to the foam so that they almost cover it.

Among the sunray place small pieces of *Leucodendron brunia* to give a contrasting texture. These, along with the sunray, should virtually fill the basket.

Next, bunch together some fluffy heads of rabbit's or hare's tail grass. Keep them taller than the other flowers so that, when slotted in, they rise above the outline.

Finally, make some little bows from pink satin ribbon (following the instructions on page 9) and place one bow on each side of the basket. All three baskets are completed in exactly the same way.

Once the three baskets are finished, tie a piece of co-ordinating cord to each basket handle. Tie all the cords together at the top so that the baskets hang one beneath the other and complete with another pink satin bow.

These tiny pot-pourri bags are so easy to create, and they make delightful gifts. Take a length of cotton fabric and, using a plate as a pattern, cut out a circle about 25-30cm (10-12in) in diameter. Hem the edge with running stitch, leaving long tails of thread at either end. Cup the fabric circle in your hand as shown and fill it with pot-pourri.

Gather the fabric into a tight ball by pulling the threads. Secure with a knot. Wire together a small tight bunch of helichrysum (strawflower or everlasting) using fine silver florists' wire and attach the posy to the bag, threading the wire through the fabric on both sides to secure. (Use a needle to make holes in the fabric first if necessary.)

Make a double bow out of satin ribbon (following the instructions on page 9) and wire this on to the bag. Finally, cut a length of gold cord about 35cm (15in) long and tie it round the posy, finishing with a double knot. Tie the ends of the cords at the desired length and hang the bag by this loop.

This fragrant string of pot-pourri bags, designed to hang in the bedroom, makes a delightful gift. First take a square of fabric and, craddling it in the palm of your hand, fill the centre with pot-pourri. Then gather the edges together, turning them in as you do so to make a wide 'hem'. Secure the fabric with wire, making a small ball. Repeat two or more times.

For each bag, make a double bow out of two lengths of wide satin ribbon, tying the second bow round the centre of the first. Gather a few delicate flowers into a small bouquet and wire the stems firmly together. Shown here are deep pink rabbit's or hare's tail grass, some large — and small — flowered helichrysum (strawflower or everlasting) and blue nipplewort (or broom bloom).

Wire the bunch around the neck of a pot-pourri bag and attach the bow, either with wire or a short length of ribbon. Repeat for the other bags. Finally, take a length of cord and tie the balls together at regular intervals.

Use some foam spheres, flowers and fabric to make this pretty mobile. Take five spheres of florists' foam. Then cut five circles of fabric, large enough to cover the balls and allowing extra to be gathered up. Experiment with a piece of paper first to determine the correct size of the circle. Wrap each piece of fabric around a ball and secure at the top with silver wire.

Make five small posies from pale blue helichrysum and nipplewort (or broom bloom). Tie the posies with silver wire, leaving a short tail which can then be pushed into the neck of the sphere. Next, cut five lengths of thin cord or ribbon and wind around the top of each ball. Tie a piece of matching ribbon around the neck of the balls and finish with a bow.

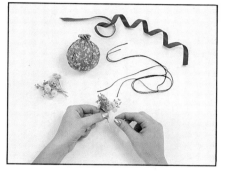

These attractive baskets filled with pot-pourri will look very pretty hanging from the dressing table, adding colour and fragrance to your bedroom. Choose a couple of miniature baskets with narrow handles. Head some pink acroclinium (sunray) and glue them round the rim of the baskets. Position them in an uneven ring to make room for the other flowers.

Fill in with heads of larkspur and purple statice, alternating the colours. Glue some of the flower heads half way up the handle on either side.

Wire more of the same flowers into bunches and stick them into a small piece of florists' foam to form a ball of flowers. Tie two pieces of dowling together at the centre with thin cord; leave two long tails of cord for hanging the mobile. Hang four bundles from the arms of the mobile, the fifth from the centre. Attach the floral 'pomander' by a longer cord from the centre.

When the rim is completely covered and the glue dry, make a double bow out of narrow pink ribbon (following the instructions on page 9) and wire it to the top of the handle. Tie a second length of wider, contrasting ribbon around the centre of the bow, leaving long tails for hanging the basket. Finally, fill the basket with pot-pourri.

I n this attractive arrangement, peachy coloured flowers set off a small brass trinket box to perfection. Cut a section from a cylinder of florists' foam to fit inside the box and secure with a strip of florists' tape.

Build up the shape of the display with cluster-flowered sunray and a few strands of creamy nipplewort (or broom bloom). The latter will add a fluffy softness to the arrangement.

T he perfect Easter present — an attractive egg-shaped gift box filled with a mass of pretty flowers. The flowers have been specially chosen to reflect the colours of the box, creating a very co-ordinated effect. Cut a section from a sphere of florists' foam and put it in the base. Secure it with tape. Place the lid about a third of the way across the foam and again tape in place.

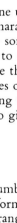

Build up the outline using brown grass and green amaranthus (love-lies-bleeding). Use some of the amaranthus leaves to add contrast of texture. Intersperse the display with a few small bunches of tiny red helichrysum, placing them well into the arrangement to give depth.

Next add the focal flowers which are peachy South African daisies (a type of helichrysum). Wire them in small groups and intersperse them throughout. Finish off with a few cones to add an interesting contrast of colour and texture.

To finish, dot a number of South African daisies (a form of helichrysum) throughout the arrangement. Provided the stems are strong, these can be added singly without wiring.

A delicate posy of dried flowers provides a perfect decoration for any gift. Choose a selection of brightly coloured, small-headed flowers and tie them together with fine wire. The flowers used here are blue larkspur, yellow South African daisy, (a type of helichrysum), small red roses and a touch of golden rod. Wrap a strip of white ribbon around the stems and finish off with a bow.

The posy on this gift box is made up in a similar way, using flowers in a range of colours that match those of the box. The posy contains green amaranthus (love-lies-bleeding), mauve xeranthemums, pink gypsophila (baby's breath), blue larkspur, cream 'caulifower' and yellow dudinea.

Attach the posies to the gifts with glue. Alternatively you can wire them on. To do this you will need to pierce two small holes in the side of the box. Wrap wire round the stems of the posy and thread it through the holes; secure on the inside.

This pretty miniature display, arranged in a tiny gift box, would make a delightful present. And with all that lavender, it smells as lovely as it looks. First cut a small block of florists' foam and pop it inside the box. Then wire a couple of red ribbons.

Wire together bunches of lavender and pack them into the foam, keeping the arrangement tallest in the middle and splaying it out at the sides. Now scatter tiny, daisy-like glixia or grass daisies throughout; push some deep into the display. Finish off by attaching the two red bows, one to the box, the other higher up on a stem of lavender.

A scallop shell makes an ideal setting for this pretty miniature arrangement. Cut a small block of florists' foam and place it in the bottom of one of the shell halves, securing it with florists' fixative or glue. Position a second shell on top and glue the two shells firmly together as shown.

Wire small clumps of pink gypsophila (baby's breath) and red nipplewort (or broom bloom). Pack them into the florists' foam, forming the outline of the arrangement. Allow a few strands of gypsophila to trail over the edge of the shell.

Three scallop shells provide the perfect setting for a colourful miniature arrangement. First you must carefully bore a hole in the base of each shell using a braddle. Now fix the shells together with wire, fanning two of them out as shown and using the third as a base. Slice a section off a sphere of florists' foam and cut it to fit the base of the shells. Glue the foam in position.

Add several wired strands of blue-dyed *Leucodendron brunia* to provide a strong contrast in colour, and finish off with two or three pieces of red amaranthus (love-lies-bleeding).

Cut off a number of honesty (silver dollar plant) seedheads and insert them singly into the foam, covering it completely. Next add small wired bunches of tiny red roses, concentrating them in the middle. Follow with clumps of golden quaking grass, positioning them so that they fan out from the centre of the arrangement and form a star-shaped outline.

Fill in amongst the quaking grass with clumps of bright yellow cluster-flowered helichrysum (strawflower or everlasting), packing them tightly into the arrangement.

DESERT ISLAND

ON THE SEASHORE

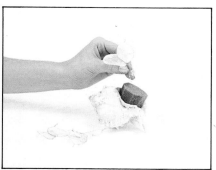

O nce again scallops have been used as the setting for a display, this time in conjunction with a 'fan' of coral to follow through the marine theme. Carefully bore a hole in the base of each shell using a braddle and fix the shells together in an open position with wire. Tape a block of florists' foam into the base and begin to build up the fan with pieces of rust coloured coral.

T he colours of this small conch have been cleverly picked out in the soft pinks and creams of the delicate arrangement. First cut a small block of florists' foam and wedge it into the neck of the shell. Then wire up a few seedheads of honesty (silver dollar plant) and position them in the foam.

Next insert several large heads of soft pink helichrysum (strawflower or everlasting). Fill in any gaps with bunches of small white helichrysum.

Now fill in using wired clumps of cluster-flowered sunray and cream anaphalis, keeping them much shorter than the coral and covering most of the foam. Allow fluffy strands of sunray to spill over the rim of the base shell.

Finally, wire together small bunches of pink rabbit's or hare's tails grass and intersperse them among the arrangement so that they stand up above the other flowers, softly breaking through the outline.

Insert two or three long-eared pods deep into the arrangement to add depth and interest. Finally add the focal flowers by positioning tight groups of South African daisies (a form of helichrysum). Peachy coloured ones have been chosen here to blend with the soft tones of the coral.

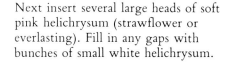

These miniature arrangements make pretty novelties to hang on the Christmas tree. One of them is made with cinnamon sticks. Take about three sticks and bind them together with wire. Wire on a double bow made out of gold gift wrap ribbon (following the instructions on page 9) and then add a posy of cones and small red helichrysum (strawflower or everlasting).

To make the other arrangement, first spray a small basket and some walnuts with gold paint. When these are dry, fill the basket with a block of florists' foam. Pack the foam with gold coloured South African daisies (a type of helichrysum) to form a spherical shape.

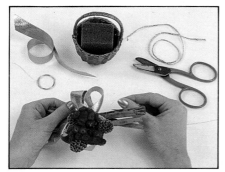

Push a length of wire through one end of each of the walnuts. Insert three or four nuts into the display, pushing them deep down amongst the flowers. Wire a small bow and attach it to the handle. Finally, hang each arrangement by means of a loop of gold cord.

Here are two more colourful decorations to hang on the Christmas tree. For the red ball, take a length of cord and wire the ends together, forming a loop. Push the wire right the way through a sphere of florists' foam and double it back on itself — into the foam — to secure. Now cover the foam with flowers.

Pack the flowers tightly into the foam to maintain the spherical shape. Those used here are deep red helichrysum (strawflower or everlasting). Fill in with little clumps of red nipplewort (or broom bloom). To finish, gather up and wire small pieces of silver netting, then insert them amongst the flowers.

For this design wire together a few flowers, such as these small white helichrysum and blue-dyed *Leucodendron brunia,* and attach three decorative bells. Gather up a piece of red netting and bind it on to the flowers. Make a double red bow as described on page 9, tie a long piece of ribbon round the middle (by which to hang the decoration) and attach the bow to the netting.

To make this splendid Christmas centrepiece, take a flat circular base such as a cake board and glue a cone of florists' foam to the centre. Then glue or staple a length of gold netting round the edge of the base, gathering it into bunches as you go. Crumple lengths of red fabric or ribbon into double loops and wire the ends. Arrange them in a ring on top of the gold.

Spray a number of Chinese lanterns and lotus seedheads with gold paint. When they are dry, wire the ends and insert them evenly spaced into the cone. Intersperse several long-eared pods throughout, pushing · them deep into the arrangement. Add highlights with a few honesty seedheads (silver dollar plant). Then wire together bunches of small red helichrysum (strawflower or everlasting) and dot them among the other plants, adding colour throughout. Finish off by inserting a few groups of white leaf skeletons — about two to three leaves per group.

Add style to the dinner table this Christmas with a striking centrepiece. Take a flat circular base — a cork mat or cake base will do — and glue single ruscus leaves around the edge. Stick three blocks of florists' foam on top, keep one taller than the others. Now insert the red candles into the foam, cutting them down as necessary to vary their heights.

Build up the arrangement using gold-sprayed poppy heads, white helichrysum (strawflower or everlasting) and more ruscus leaves. The white adds essential highlights to the arrangement. Finish off by scattering single red roses throughout the display. The colours chosen here are especially for Christmas, but for other times of the year you can choose different colours.

This attractive 'woodland' design makes the perfect centrepiece for a stripped pine table. Begin by making a base out of three large dried leaves, such as these cobra leaves. Glue the leaves together, then glue a block of florists' foam on top. Wire up several cones and walnuts, forcing the wire through the base of the nuts as far as it will go.

Wire together clumps of oak leaves and build up the outline of the display. Now insert the nuts and cones, placing the former in small groups. Keep the shape irregular to make it more interesting. Brighten the display by scattering small clumps of ammobium (sandflower or winged everlasting) throughout. To finish, trim a candle to the required length and push it into the foam.

A pair of candlestick holders is transformed by a tightly-packed arrangement of dried flowers. For each stick, cut a sphere of florist's foam in half and hollow out the centre of each piece so that the foam sits snugly round the stem. Wrap a piece of florists' tape around the two halves to hold them together.

Push short stems of orange South African daisy (a form of helichrysum) into the foam, keeping the arrangement spherical. Then fill in with small wired clumps of red helichrysum (strawflower or everlasting) and pink miniature sunray, being sure not to leave any gaps.

Create some pretty coasters using a few flowers and some mother-of-pearl discs. The latter can be bought from any shop specializing in shells. They should measure at least 4cm (1½in) more than the diameter of your glass base. Choose any combination of flowers or seedheads — shown above are helichrysum, honesty and hydrangea. Cut the heads off the plants.

Now create a ring around the edge of a shell by gluing the heads in position. The honesty (silver dollar plant) can be stuck down first — the heads slightly overlapping — and the red helichrysum can be glued down on top at regular intervals. If you are only using helichrysum, alternate the colours for a more interesting effect.

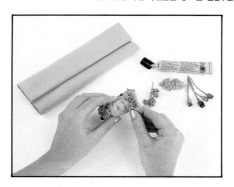

Try decorating some wooden napkin rings with a few dried flowers. You can either cover the ring entirely or make a pretty posy to tie on top. To do the former, simply cover the ring in glue. Then stick masses of tiny flowers on to it until the whole surface is covered. The flowers used here are yellow helichrysum, beige cluster-flowered sunray and poppy seedheads.

To make the posy gather a small square of pink spotted netting in the middle with a long piece of silver wire. Using the same wire, secure strands of beard grass on to the back of the netting, on either side as shown. Next add two pieces of coral, wiring them on in the same way. Finish off by arranging some South African daisies (helichrysum) and cluster-flowered sunray to the front.

Use plenty of fluffy cluster-flowered sunray to hide the wire. Finish off by tying the posy on to the ring with a length of white cord. In this way, by simply untying the cord, each of your supper guests can take home a small memento.

Dried flowers always enhance the dining table, especially when they are used so prettily to decorate the napkins. Buy a length of satin ribbon, choosing a colour to match (or, if you prefer, contrast) that of your napkins. Wire together a small bunch of flowers with silver wire; this posy contains bleached white nipplewort, a couple of long-eared pods and a single red rose.

Take about 35cm (14in) of ribbon per napkin and cut a V-shape in each end. Wrap ribbon round the stalk of the posy and tie a knot at the back, leaving one end longer than the other. Form a loop with the long end (for the napkin to go through) and tie a second knot. Bring the ends to the front of the posy and form a bow. The arrangement can now be put on the napkin.

A ball of colourful flowers adds a welcome splash of colour to an old wooden lamp stand. Begin by slicing a sphere of florists' foam in half and cutting away the centre of each half so that the pieces fit snugly around the stand. Tape the two halves in position as shown.

Wire the flowers into small bunches; used here are blue larkspur, small yellow helichrysum (strawflower or everlasting), green amaranthus (love-lies-bleeding) and dudinea. Insert the plants into the foam, keeping the shape spherical. Position the more spiky larkspur and amaranthus first, then fill in with the dudinea and helichrysum.

A striking and imaginative display transforms a plain lampshade. Begin by wiring together three bunches of flowers, carefully selecting plants that blend well with the colour of your shade. The plants shown here are helichrysum (strawflower or everlasting), cluster-flowered sunray and rat's tail statice.

Make three small holes at the base of the shade. Attach the bunches on to the shade by threading the wires through the holes and securing them at the back. Position the middle bunch upright and the ones on either side running parallel with the rim. Make sure the ends are packed closely together so that none of the stems or wires is showing.

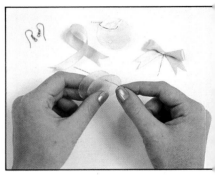

Make your own ear-rings out of dried flowers and mother-of-pearl. The fittings can be bought in a craft shop or good department store, the mother-of-pearl from any shop specializing in shells. For each ear-ring, take two shell discs and pierce a hole through the top of each using a needle. Now thread the ear-ring pin through the holes, and bend it into a loop.

Using silver wire, bind together a small bunch of pink-dyed gypsophila (baby's breath) and a couple of honesty seedheads (silver dollar plant). Make a small pink bow out of satin ribbon and wire it round the posy.

Why not decorate your hair on a sunny day with this pretty hair slide? To begin, wire the plants individually; shown here are small pink helichrysum (strawflower or everlasting), South African daisies (also helichrysum), moon grass, leaf skeletons and small cones. Then tie them into a bunch by gradually binding them together with a single piece of silver wire.

To finish simply glue the bunch on to a plastic hair slide using an all-purpose adhesive.

Glue the bunch on to the shells with an all-purpose adhesive. Alternatively, you can make a small hole at the bottom of the disc and wire the posy in position. Finally, attach the discs on to the ear-ring fitting using the looped pin.

A small straw hat, decorated with a garland of dried flowers, makes a pretty design to hang on the bedroom wall. This particular hat is a small doll's hat. Begin by making three bows out of satin ribbon, as described on page 9. Tie a second length of ribbon round the middle of one of the bows to form the long 'tails' at the back of the hat.

Make a garland to wrap around the crown as follows. Attach some fine florists' wire to a length of string, about 20-25cm (8-10in) from one end. Place a small bunch of flowers over the join and secure with the wire. Add another bunch to cover the stems of the first and bind as before. Continue adding to the garland in this way until it is the desired length.

The flowers used in this garland are red amaranthus (love-lies-bleeding), South African daisy (helichrysum) and golden dryandra. Wrap the garland round the crown and tie the ends of the string together to secure. Wire a couple of bows to the front of the hat and put the other one over the join at the back.

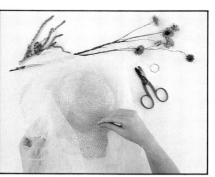

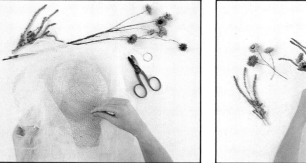

Cut a dash in this stunning and original design made simply from a plain straw hat and just two varieties of flower. First cut a length of pink netting, long enough to wind around the crown of the hat and leave a modest train. Gather the net loosely round the hat and either stitch or wire the fabric to the front and back of the crown.

Using silver wire, tie together a bunch of acroclinium (sunray) and long stems of rat's tail statice. Attach the flowers to the back of the hat, winding the wire securely around the netting. To finish, make a double bow with long trailing tails out of pink satin ribbon — following instructions on page 9. Attach the bow to the hat, using it to cover up any wire that still shows.

Even a small courtyard garden can yield a wide range of annuals, perennials, shrubs and trees to provide flowers and foliage to press.

The way nature has fashioned flowers gives us great but short-lived pleasure and delight; capture this delight by pressing flowers and you will have the perfect medium for creating pictures of lasting beauty. To enjoy collecting and pressing you do not have to act like a botanist seeking specimens, but your enjoyment of the countryside will increase as you start to look more closely at what is growing there. Examine the structure of each flower you find and learn to appreciate, for instance, the beauty in a single floret of cow parsley or the exquisite detail in the veining of a rose leaf. Try also to learn the plants' names. You will soon discover which plants are most suitable for pressing and when best to pick them, and to help you, we have illustrated many of the most suitable and colourful ones on page 55.

GATHERING WILD FLOWERS

There is an amazing variety of wild flowers, many of which you may have never previously noticed, and if you gather sparingly from the countryside, you will not harm the plant's future growth. However, do pay attention to the official list of protected and endangered plants that you may not pick. Don't break off stems or pull up roots, but cleanly cut the parts you require with scissors. If you place the cut flowers in an opaque plastic carrier bag, blow it up like a balloon and seal it, they will keep well for a few hours. Don't forget also to gather leaves, tendrils, stems, grasses and seedheads. Among the best leaves are those of carrot, meadowsweet, cow parsley, rose, wild strawberry, silverweed, vetch, cherry, maple, sumach and virginia creeper.

FLOWERS TO GROW OR BUY

Annuals, perennials, shrubs and trees all provide material for pressing and, even if you only have a window box, you can sow alyssum, candytuft, forget-me-knot, lobelia and polyanthus. Succulent and fleshy flowers contain too much moisture to press successfully. Multi-petalled or thick centred flowers such as roses, carnations, chrysanthemums and marguerites do not press satisfactorily as whole flowers but need to be broken into separate parts for pressing.

When picking flowers from the garden, lay them gently in a basket as you cut them, and then dry and press them as soon as possible.

You can still find flowers to press on wet days and in the winter months by visiting a florist where you can purchase a wide range of cut flowers, foliage and pot plants.

WHEN TO PICK AND PRESS

The optimum time to pick flowers is at midday when all the dew has evaporated. Sunny weather is best and rainy days should be avoided. If you have to pick flowers in damp weather, pick whole stems, and stand them indoors in water for a few hours until the flowerheads are dry. Pick flowers at their best, when they have just opened (and before they produce pollen), and gather some buds as well. Look out for varying sizes, unusual shapes, a variety of tints and veining, and interesting visual textures. Remember as you are pressing that you can thin out collective flowerheads such as spiraea, candytuft, wild parsley (Queen Ann's lace) and hydrangea, so do not pass over large headed flowers.

Bought flowers also need immediate attention, so don't be tempted to enjoy their beauty for a few days before pressing, but press them while they are at their best.

Pressed flower arranging need not be an expensive hobby: the design elements (i.e. the flowers) can cost nothing and the equipment is relatively cheap; you can even make your own press at no great expense (see page 54). The amount of money you spend on a design depends largely on the cost of your setting.

Glassine photographic negative bags are ideal for storing your flowers as they are made from acid-free paper which will not attack the plant material. Aids for handling the flowers include a palette knife, tweezers and a paint brush. Miniature flowers like alyssum can be picked up with a needle point and moved about with a fine paint brush. Larger flowers can be picked up with a palette knife or a slightly dampened finger tip and then transferred to the grip of round-nosed tweezers. To fix flowers in a design use latex adhesive. Squeeze a small amount of adhesive on to a palette dish and use a cocktail stick or toothpick to transfer a small dot of it on to the centre back of a flower. Now press the flower in position.

Sprays and larger flowers may need several dots of adhesive to hold them in place, although great care must be taken to ensure that no adhesive can be seen from the front of the flower as this will ruin the finished look of your design. You should discard the latex as soon as it starts to set in the dish and replace it with a fresh supply.

THE DESIGN BASE

All pictures must be formed on some base; this can be paper, fabric, wood, metal or plastic, and in this book it is referred to as the design base. In choosing textiles, remember that some man-made fabrics are unsuitable in both texture and colour. Old satins and silks are excellent, as are the range of velvets and fine cottons.

Art shops carry a great range of papers and boards. As a design base for pictures, parchment, marbled and watercolour papers are highly suitable. Rough textured watercolour papers and the many shades of heavyweight Ingres paper and twin-wire self-coloured boards are equally suitable for making greeting cards. To make a card, first cut a rectangle of paper or board to the required size, then score (make a crease) along the fold line. To score the card, lay it face down on a cutting board and, using a blunt instrument such as a knitting needle or the blunt edge of a scissor blade, 'rule' firmly down the edge of a ruler. You can now easily fold along this line; if necessary trim the card after it has been folded. Before drawing on the card with a coloured pen it is advisable to mark out your border first in pencil.

Shown below is a range of the equipment you will need for making pressed flower designs. It includes: 1) latex adhesive; 2) cocktail sticks; 3) palette knife; 4) round-nosed tweezers; 5) assorted paint brushes; 6) ruler; 7) pencil; 8) compass; 9) coloured marker pens; 10) varnish; 11) large and small fine scissors; 12) craft knife and, of course, flowers 13).

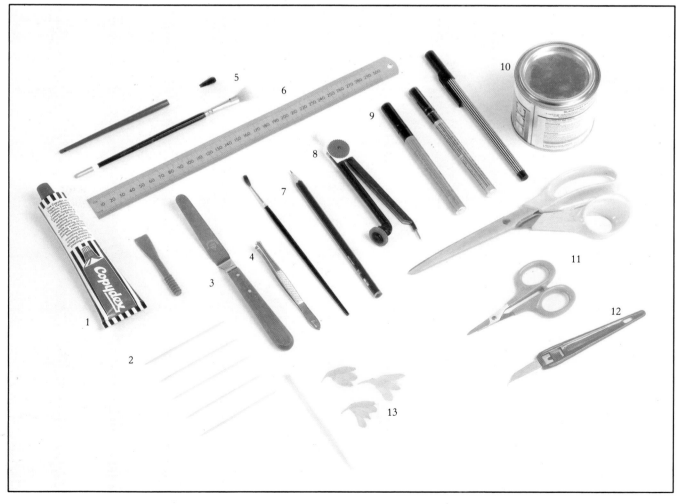

Large flowers can be picked up on the end of a slightly moistened finger tip before being gripped and moved about with round-nosed tweezers.

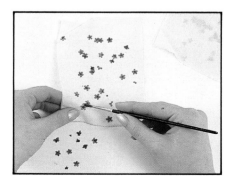

After pressing, small flowers can be removed from the tissue by bending the paper round a finger and lifting the flowers off with a paint brush.

Pressed flower designs should always be protected to prevent damage from handling, humidity, exposure to the atmosphere and, as far as possible, from ultraviolet light. Humidity makes pressed flowers curl and exposure to air makes the colours oxidize and quickly fade. To avoid damage from ultraviolet light, which will also bleach colours, all designs should be kept away from direct sunlight, and as glass or acetate will also act as an ultraviolet filter, perhaps the most satisfactory protection is to have the design tightly sealed and covered by a sheet of glass or rigid plastic. As this is not practical in every application, other solutions have been found.

SEALING TECHNIQUES

Much of your early work will probably be in the form of greeting cards, and these require a light and flexible covering for the design. Self-adhesive, protective 'library film' is available in rolls with either a gloss or matt finish. It is easy to cut, and after some practice, to smooth over the design. Practise applying library film on a few flower groups of various thickness before you attempt a finished design. Cut a generous piece of film to cover your design, then pull away one edge of the backing paper. Position the film over the design and carefully begin to rub it down with a soft cloth, gradually pulling back the backing paper as you go. The film will need particularly careful rubbing down over thick flowers to avoid trapping air bubbles. When you have finished, trim off any excess film.

Where the greeting card involves an outer card used as a 'mount' for the inner design card, an acetate 'window' can be fixed in position over the aperture (see below), in a way that both enhances the card and protects the pressed flower design beneath.

A slightly heavier and more durable material than library film is 'iron-on' protective film, and again this is available in gloss and matt finishes, and also in a 'linen weave' finish which is ideal for the table mat applications (see page 83). It is a little more expensive than the smooth-on type, and requires some practice (and not too much heat), but it does 'bond' to both flowers and base material very well and the finish gives a professional 'laminated' look.

When decorating objects such as wooden boxes or glass jars, the best way to seal the design is to cover it with several coats of varnish, either matt polyurethane or one of the new ultra hard 'two pack' types, depending on the base material. In these instances, the varnish can also be used to fix the flowers on to the design.

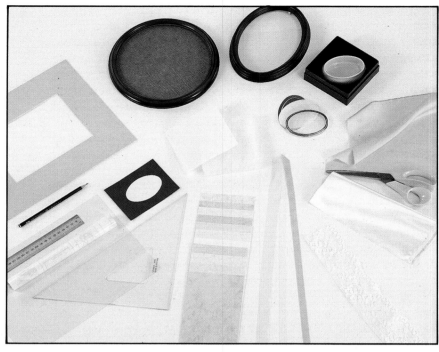

Items used in mounting and framing designs include picture frames, boxes with lids designed to hold craftwork, silks and satin for the design base, ribbons and lace, design papers, acetate sheets, self adhesive 'library' film, a set square, ruler and pencil, and wadding and foam sheets.

When choosing a picture frame to display pressed flower work, it is most important to make sure that the rebate in the frame (the recess which holds the glass) is deep enough to accept not only the glass, a thin mount, the design paper and the picture back, but also the wadding or foam material that is used to apply pressure to keep the flowers in contact with the glass. The picture back itself must be made of hardboard or plywood, as cardboard will not be strong enough to apply sufficient pressure. The glass must fit accurately into its frame, so that air is, to a great extent, excluded. Recommended wadding material is either synthetic wadding of the sort used in dress making, or the thin plastic foam sheeting used in upholstery. Both are equally suitable, but the depth of the rebate in the frame will decide which is best for each application.

When covering an aperture in a greeting card, apply a line of 'impact' adhesive around the cut-out and, while it is still wet, cover with an acetate sheet.

To cover a design with protective film, gradually pull away the backing paper and rub the film down with a soft cloth, being careful to avoid air bubbles.

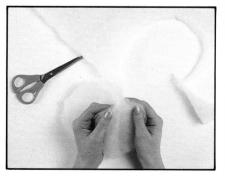

Use wadding, as employed in dress making, to pad out frames. It can easily be cut to the correct shape, and a layer pulled off if it is too thick.

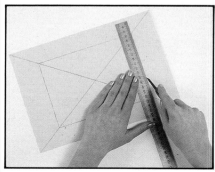

To centre the aperture on a mount, draw an 'X' on the reverse of the mount as shown, then draw your aperture with its corners touching the diagonals.

If you have decided that your picture will be enhanced by a mount, it is advisable to prepare this before starting on your design. An artist's watercolour is often set off by a rebated mount, but in a pressed flower picture, unlike a watercolour, you must have the surface of the picture pressed tightly against the glass. If you wish to use a rebated mount, arrange the design on fine fabric which can be pressed through the thickness of the mount by a piece of wadding, cut to fit the aperture (see Victoriana on page 67). If the design material is paper or card, the mount itself should be made of thin paper, and lines can be ruled on it to give an impression of depth.

────────── THE FRAMING SEQUENCE. ──────────

The sequence of framing a pressed flower picture depends on the material on which the flowers are being arranged. If it is paper or board, then all the framing work can be done after the picture has been completed, but if it is silk or other woven material, then all the backing material must be in place before work on arranging the flowers is started.

When working with woven material, take the picture back out of the frame and clean it carefully to remove dust and loose particles. Cut a piece of wadding and a piece of your chosen fabric just a little smaller than the back. Lay the back on your work table, centre the wadding on it, and cover with the fabric. If the picture is to have a mount around it, cut the wadding to fit the aperture. When the picture composition is complete, use a dry paint brush to clear away unwanted particles from the base material. Accurately position the mount, carefully lay the cleaned picture glass over it and then lower the frame itself over the glass. Slip your fingers under the picture back, keeping pressure on the frame, turn it over and place it on a soft surface. Now, while still keeping pressure on the back, use a small hammer to gently tack fine panel pins into the frame to hold the back in place. A heavy duty staple gun could be used, but remember that too much vibration at this stage may dislodge some of your carefully arranged flowers. Finally, use picture tape or high-tack masking tape to seal the back and cover the nail heads. Ordinary clear cellulose tape is not suitable as the adhesive dries out, it is not waterproof, and is inclined to shrink. When using rigid, rather than woven, material it is easier to pick up the finished design, lay this on top of the previously prepared wadding and picture back, and then follow the same framing procedures as described above.

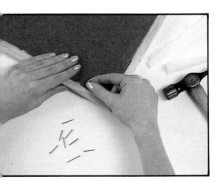

When securing the picture back, keep applying local pressure while you carefully hammer in fine panel pins every 75mm (3in).

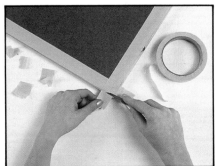

When the back is fully secured, use high-tack masking or picture frame tape to seal the gap. This excludes the air and covers the nail heads.

Once pressed, the form of a flower loses its third dimension. So when planning a design, rather than following the guidelines of three-dimensional flower arranging, you should try to create a two-dimensional representation as in a painting.

Look at the designs on the following pages and study the colour, shape and texture of each one. Then look further into the proportions, balance and rhythm of each design. Learn from the harmonizing shades and hues of Falling Leaves on page 61, the contrast of shape, colour and texture of Lazy Daisy on page 58, the mood of cool simplicity of Eastern Inspiration on page 73, the perfect symmetry of Victorian Posy on page 65 and the delicate miniature work of Crystal Miniature on page 79 and the brooch and pendants on page 92. And when you have copied some of these designs, maybe you will be ready to let your personal creativity take over and become an innovator of fresh ideas.

When creating your own designs, spend time choosing your flowers and foliage, carefully considering the colour and shape of each item. Consider also the size and shape of your mount or frame, and decide what shape your design is to take — the line drawings below, illustrating some basic shapes and their focal points, can be used as guidelines. Try to be confident and fix each flower straight down on to the design base rather than move it about from one place to another first — overhandling the flowers will damage their delicate structure.

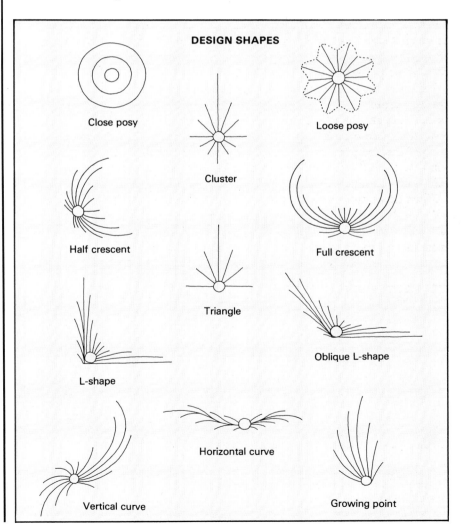

DESIGN SHAPES

Close posy

Cluster

Loose posy

Half crescent

Full crescent

Triangle

L-shape

Oblique L-shape

Horizontal curve

Vertical curve

Growing point

MAKING A PRESS

To make your own press, cut two pieces of 10mm (³/₈in) plywood measuring 275mm (10¾in) square. Clamp them together and drill 5mm (³/₁₆in) holes in each corner, 18mm (¾in) from the sides. Open up the holes in the top square to 8mm (⁵/₁₆in). Sand all surfaces, rounding the corners, and apply two coats of matt varnish.

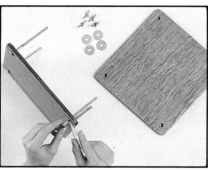

Purchase some 7mm by 200mm (¼in by 8in) fully threaded bolts, with washers and wing-nuts (if not available you can use shorter bolts, 150mm (6in) long). The holes drilled in the bottom square are slightly undersize, but the bolts can be screwed in; add a little 'super' strong glue to the bottom threads just before screwing the bolts home, to fix them permanently.

Take some old newspapers and some thin, double-walled corrugated cardboard and cut them into rectangles 225mm by 255mm (9in by 10in). Cut sheets of blotting paper to the same size then assemble the press by sandwiching layers of blotting paper and newspaper between the cardboard. Each cardboard 'sandwich' should contain 12 sheets of newspaper with two sheets of blotting paper in the centre.

HOW TO PRESS FLOWERS

Small flowers and leaves should be placed face down on smooth toilet tissue on top of the blotting paper. Cover them with more tissue before covering with another sheet of blotting paper. Pick sprays of small flowers and press a few whole, but snip off the individual heads of the majority and arrange in rows on the toilet tissue as shown, using a paint brush to move them into position.

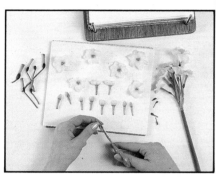

Larger flowers such as narcissus 'Sol d'Or' can be placed directly on to the blotting paper, having cut away all the harder parts with sharp scissors. Flowers pressed in profile need to be cut in half lengthways. Put a tab sticking out from between the layers in the press to identify what flowers you have in that layer or layers, and the date when they were put in.

Multi-petalled flowers such as roses and carnations must be broken down into separate petals before pressing and depending on their size, should be pressed directly between either blotting paper or toilet tissue. The stems, sepals and bracts should be pressed separately in a press devoted to thick items. Use twice as much newspaper as usual between the layers in this press.

Not all leaves are suitable for pressing (see page 50), and of those that are, usually only the younger ones are used. An exception is autumn coloured leaves which often have part of their water content already removed naturally, due to the season. As with flowers, cut or pull the leaves from the stems and arrange neatly on the paper. If they are thick, put them in a press reserved for such material.

Remove all unwanted material from the blossom of trees and shrubs before pressing the flowers. Cut the backs off trumpet shaped flowers when pressing flat, but leave the bloom whole when it is being pressed in profile. When you have finished preparing the press, put the lid on and tighten down gently. At first, tighten the press daily then less frequently until, between six and eight weeks, the plants are dry.

This beautiful design displays some of the most suitable and certainly the most colourful flowers used for pressing.

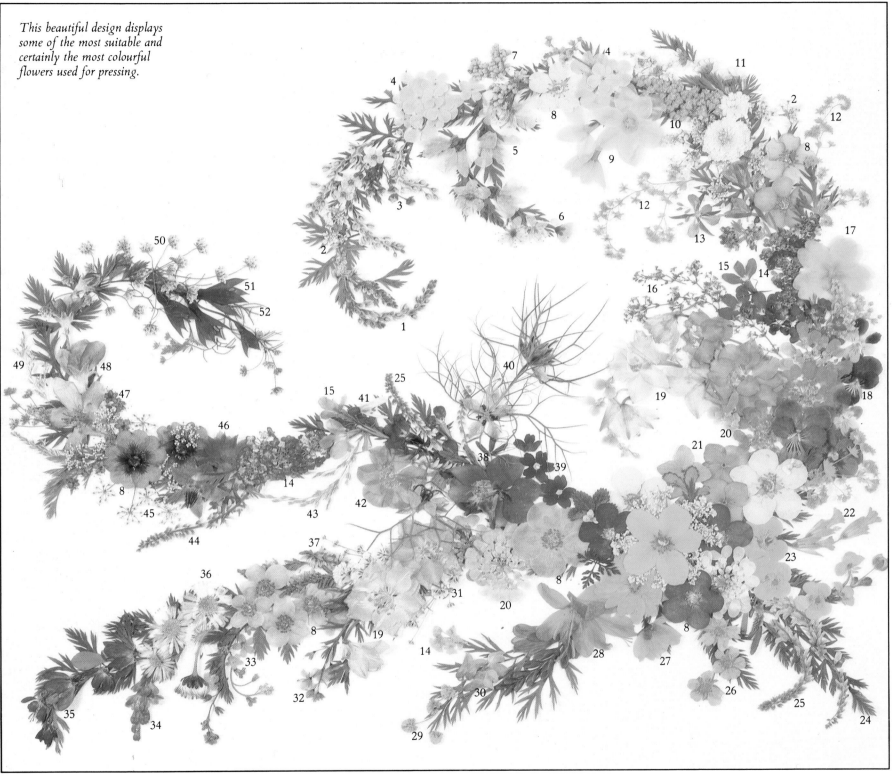

1) Russian (silver lace) vine **2)** Fools' parsley **3)** Spring flowering spiraea **4)** Guelder rose (cranberry bush) **5)** Whitebeam blossom **6)** Blackthorn blossom
7) Meadowsweet **8)** Potentilla **9)** Narcissus Sol d'Or **10)** Golden rod
11) Feverfew **12)** Lady's mantle **13)** Rose bay willow herb **14)** Alyssum **15)** Lobelia
16) Lady's bedstraw **17)** Primrose **18)** Pansy **19)** Larkspur **20)** Candytuft
21) Hydrangea **22)** Cowslip **23)** Buttercup **24)** Carrot leaves **25)** Melilot

26) Creeping cinquefoil **27)** Kerria **28)** Montbretia **29)** Hop trefoil **30)** Horsehoe vetch **31)** Gypsophila (baby's breath) **32)** Speedwell **33)** Forget-me-not
34) Flowering currant **35)** Japanese crab apple **36)** Daisy **37)** Heather
38) Delphinium **39)** Verbena **40)** Love-in-a-mist **41)** Snowdrop **42)** Rock rose
43) Bent grass **44)** Borage **45)** Cow parsley **46)** Cornflower **47)** Spiraea **48)** Apple blossom **49)** Creeping bent grass **50)** Chervil **51)** Fuchsia **52)** Smoke bush (smoketree).

This card will bring your Valentine a heart 'full of flowers'. Cut a rectangle of pale blue cardboard 400mm by 200mm (16in by 8in); crease and fold it in half. With a craft knife and ruler, cut out a 128mm (5in) square from the centre of the front page. Cut four pieces of lace to fit the sides of this cut-out, mitre the corners and glue in position. Fix a square of acetate to the inside of the 'window'.

Also cut, crease and fold a white card to the above size. On the front page lightly mark out a 'heart' in pencil, to fit within the 'window', adding a few lines to break into the heart. Take a spray of *Acaena* 'Blue Haze' foliage and fix to the right hand top of the heart. Add more leaves and tendrils at various points around the shape, using only pinpoint size dots of adhesive to secure each one to the card.

Apply a tiny dot of adhesive to the top right of the heart and, using the tip of a dry, fine paint brush, tease an alyssum flower over it. Continue to fix tiny flowers all around the heart shape, finishing at the top with a forget-me-not. When the design is complete, carefully glue around the outside edge of the design card, and fix it centrally inside the blue card. Do not glue the back page down.

White satin, flowers and the impression of a church steeple conveys all. Cut a piece of watercolour paper 185mm by 290mm (7¾in by 11½in); crease and fold it in half lengthways. Cut a triangle [base: 115mm (4½in), height: 145mm (6½in)] from the front of the card, then cut a single sheet of paper to fit inside the card; pencil the triangle shape on to it.

A garland of pink alyssum and blue forget-me-nots makes a delightful welcome card for a new baby. Cut and fold a blue (or pink) and a white piece of paper to form two cards 150mm (6in) square. Draw and cut out a 95mm (3½in) circle from the centre front of the coloured card. From this circle cut out the crib and edge it as shown with lace, sticking the lace down with glue.

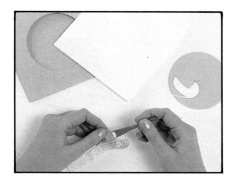

Cut 300mm (12in) of 16mm (⅝in) white satin ribbon, fold it and stick it to the apex of the triangle, leaving a loop at the top. Trim the tails to length. Cut a further 600mm (24in) and a 100mm (4in) length of ribbon. Tie a bow in the long one and form bow-like loops in the short one. Sew together and glue to the top of the triangle. Fold the ribbon ends under the card and secure.

Put the white card inside the coloured card, trim off any surplus paper and trace a feint pencil line through the circle on to the white card. Put the coloured card to one side. Glue the crib on to the centre of the white circle, then form a garland just inside the pencil line using silver southernwood leaves. Next place a cluster of pink alyssum at the quarter points.

Take the single sheet of paper and fix rose leaves and small potentillas inside the tope of the triangle. Gradually add further potentillas, gypsophila and leaves, moving down and outwards to fill the triangle. The finished look is light and spacey, giving a wedding bouquet effect. Glue a piece of acetate over the design and stick the whole sheet to the inside of the folded card.

Scatter a few forget-me-nots to gently break up the edge of the clusters. Cut a 110mm (4½in) square of white tulle and fix it using latex adhesive on to the inside front cover of the coloured card to cover the hole. Finally, apply glue sparingly all around the inside edge of the front cover and carefully stick the white card in position with the design showing through the window.

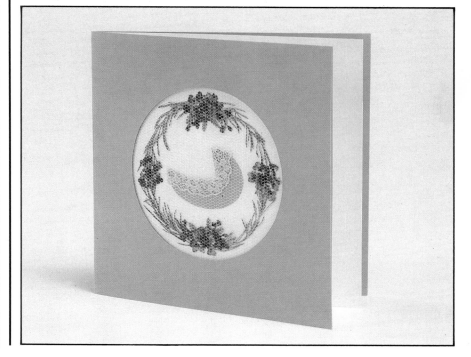

Simple daisies can make a chic greeting card. Cut some pale oyster tinted cardboard to 65mm by 165mm (2½in by 6½in). Group three daisies slightly off centre, place another one a little below and to the right and a final one to the left and above the group. Fill in with leaves and stems of hedge bedstraw. Form the focal point with florets of fools' parsley positioned on the most prominent daisy.

This buttercup card brings a ray of sunshine with its greeting. Cut some green paper to 65mm by 165mm (2½in by 6½in). Begin the arrangement with salad burnet and melilot, placing them in the top left corner and bringing them down to form a lazy 'V'. Add buttercups towards the centre, saving the most dominant for the focal point, just off centre, at the base.

Choose purple for the main card, to match the colour with the tips of the daisy petals. Cut the card to 200mm by 215mm (8in by 8½in), score and fold lengthways into a 'tent'. Carefully cover the design with protective film and trim to size. The pale design card against the dark background card will require no border rule. Measure the central position on the background card and glue down the design.

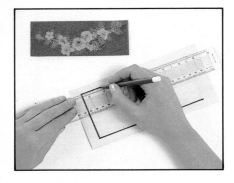

For the best effect, tuck the leaves under the focal buttercup; also ensure that the 'V' is not symmetrical. Cover the design with protective film and trim. Cut a rectangle of cream cardboard 200mm by 215mm (8in by 8½in); crease and fold it lengthways. Draw two rectangles as shown, using a green marker and making the outer rule twice as thick as the inner one. Glue the design inside the border.

Any child would be delighted to receive a pretty flower garden created in real flowers on their birthday card. From green cardboard cut a rectangle 240mm by 175mm (9½in by 7in) in size, crease it and fold it widthways. From an offcut of the green board cut out the required birthday number. Now using white cardboard cut out a rectangle 65mm by 120mm (2½in by 4¾in).

Take a large spray of meadowsweet to make the larger tree and a suitable stem for the trunk. Similarly, make a smaller tree for the other side of the number. Build up the picture by adding verbena, lobelia, cow parsley and daisies to create a colourful border. Cover the design with protective film and carefully trim to size.

Draw a border in pencil on the green card; this will house the design (the border shown is an Edwardian 'reversed corner'). When satisfied with the border, go over it with a dark green fine marker pen. Fix the design within this border.

This traditional Christmas card is easily made. Cut a rectangle of white cardboard to measure 165mm by 65mm (6½in by 2½in). Select a piece of bracken fern about 140mm (5½in) in length. Fix the bracken to the card with spots of glue. Leave sufficient space at the base of this 'tree' for the 'flower pot'. For the star, colour a floret of fools' parsley gold, and glue to the top of the tree.

From red metallic board cut a rectangle 215mm by 200mm (8½in by 8in); crease, and fold in half lengthways. Now draw a rectangle — larger than the white card — on the red card using a gold marker. Cut out a 'flower pot' from some red board, draw on some decorative lines and fix the pot to the tree. Cover the design card with protective film and fix it centrally within the gold border.

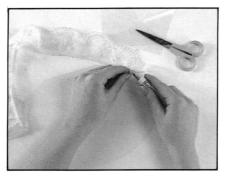

Capture the art of bygone days with this card, which can be easily converted into a calendar. From a sheet of acetate, cut an oval 180mm by 250mm (7in by 9¾in). Take one metre (about 40in) of 55mm (2½in) wide gathered cream lace, and using an 'impact' adhesive, glue the gathered edge twice around the acetate oval, about 35mm (1³/₈in) from the edge, to make a double thickness of lace.

Crease and fold in half some heavy-weight dark brown cardboard. Mark out an oval on this, the same size as the acetate, but overlapping the folded edge so that, having cut the card out, the two sheets of board are joined for 90mm (3½in) at the fold. Using sprays of Russian (silver lace) vine and leaves of cutleaf Japanese maple *Acer palmatum dissectum,* create a crescent outline on the front.

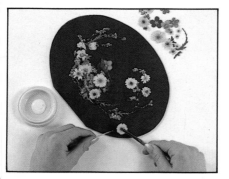

Fill in the centre and the right arm of the crescent with flowers of feverfew and peach and rust coloured potentillas, and the left arm with buds and flowers of white potentilla. Now use buds and flowers of blackthorn to break up the solidness of the larger flowers. Add interest and colour to the centre with a rock geranium and a leaf of purpleleaf Japanese maple, *Acer palmatum atropurpurea.*

Glue around the outside edge of the front page of the brown card, and fix the acetate sheet and lace centrally over it. Leave this under pressure to dry. Finally, make a small bow from 6mm (¼in) cream satin lace and fix it to the top centre. To convert to a calendar, buy a small calendar block, cover it with brown card and trim with satin ribbon. Suspend this from the main card, then glue the card together.

T his striking design is ideal for the non flowery. Cut a rectangle from brown cardboard 207mm by 510mm (8¼in by 20in); crease and fold it widthways. Make a similar card from cream cardboard. Cut an aperture in the brown card 140mm by 190mm (5½in by 7½in). Now cut an acetate sheet to 195mm by 240mm (7¾in by 9½in) and fix it inside the brown card over the aperture.

For the design card, cut a single sheet of light brown cardboard to 190mm by 230mm (7½in by 9in). Take a selection of autumn-coloured sumach leaves and, fixing with latex adhesive, make a crab-like shape. Use leaves with curling tips to give movement to the design.

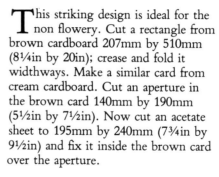

T he clever harmony of paper, shape and flowers gives this card a three-dimensional effect. Cut a rectangle of maroon coloured cardboard 230mm by 165mm (9in by 6½in) crease it and fold it in half widthways. Place a compass point 65mm (2½in) from the top of the card and in the centre; now draw a circle of 75mm (3in) in diameter and cut this out carefully.

For the centre of the design, use the reverse side of an astrantia flower to show off its beautiful veining. Fix this firmly with adhesive and finally add a floret of fennel over its stalk end. Glue this design centrally to the acetate inside the aperture and when dry, glue the cream card inside the darker brown one by its front page only. Trim off any excess cream card.

Cut and fold a sheet of grey paper (preferably imitation parchment) to fit inside the maroon card. Using a silver/mauve outline pen in the compass, describe a 56mm (2¼in) circle centrally, and 65mm (2½in) from the top of the paper, so that it will sit within the cut-out in the maroon card. Select a red potentilla, copper carpet foliage and several florets of the hebe 'Midsummer Beauty'.

On the grey paper place a spray of foliage from the centre to the top of the circle. Add more foliage at the right edge and base. Now tuck in some hebe. A potentilla at the base of the circle will form the focal point. Cut a 100mm (4in) square of acetate and fix this inside the maroon card to cover the cut-out. Glue the grey paper inside the card, to the front page, so the design is central in the aperture.

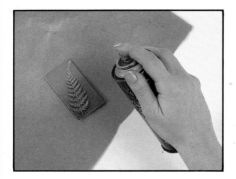

Turn offcuts of cardboard into pretty gift tags. Cut a piece each of red metallic and glossy white cardboard 75mm by 100mm (3in by 4in) and fold widthways. Secure a tip of polypody fern to the front of the red card. Spray with gold paint. When dry, lift off the fern, leaving a silhouette. Fix the gold fern to the front of the white card. Punch holes in the top left corners and thread with ribbon.

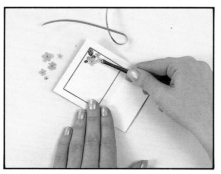

Cut a piece of single-sided glossy green cardboard 75mm by 100mm (3in by 4in). Crease and fold 40mm (1½in) from the left edge to give a folded card size of 75mm by 60mm (3in by 2½in). With a green marker pen, draw a border inside the larger page. Fix a spray of miniature rose leaves in one corner then form a loose line of guelder rose (cranberry bush) flowers up the page.

Having looked at the construction of an envelope, make a miniature version from a 140mm (5½in) square of paper. Glue the envelope together and line the side flaps with a silver marker. Take wispy foliage, gypsophila (baby's breath) and mauve lobelia and secure them inside the envelope so that they appear to be bursting out. Attach some curled mauve ribbon to the top of the tag.

Take some red and green single-sided cardboard and cut out some sock shapes. Using gold or silver aerosol paint, spray heads of fools' parsley; when dry, secure the best shaped florets to the heels and toes of the socks. Draw a ribbed border at the top of each sock, punch a small hole in the corner, and add coloured ties.

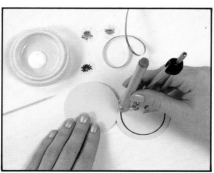

Crease and fold a small piece of yellow cardboard in half and, with your compass pencil just overlapping the fold, draw a 65mm (2½in) circle. Cut this out, leaving the card hinged together by about 30mm (1¼in) at the top. Draw a 50mm (2in) circle in green marker pen on the front cover and fix three daisies in the middle. Re-fold the card and fix a length of thin green ribbon about the fold.

MAUVE SATIN MARKER | THISTLEDOWN MARKER

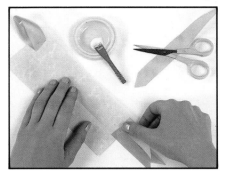

Blue delphiniums and pink candytuft are combined with mauve satin ribbon to create this most attractive bookmark. Select a piece of grey imitation parchment paper and cut a rectangle 200mm by 80mm (8in by 3¼in). Crease and fold it in half lengthways. Open up the folded parchment and on the right hand page fix a loop of 25mm (1in) wide pale mauve ribbon, using latex adhesive. Cut two pieces of ribbon 90mm (3½in) long and trim in a V-shape. Fix these to the foot of the card as shown. Turn the card over to form the design on the page opposite that bearing the ribbons.

Begin with silverweed leaves facing alternately up the page. Next fix a blue delphinium near the base and overlap with mauve candytuft. Tuck in single candytuft florets under the leaves, gradually decreasing their size up the page and finishing with a few buds. Glue the two pages of card together. Cover both sides with matt protective film (cut to the height of the bookmark and twice the width).

The mass of gypsophila (baby's breath) floating up from the bed of pink alyssum gives the impression of thistledown on the breeze. This simple design makes an attractive marker for any book. Cut a strip of black cardboard 300mm by 50mm (12in by 2in). Crease a line 75mm (3in) from the top and fold under. This forms a flap to tuck over a page. Starting about 6mm (¼in) from the base, fix clusters of pink alyssum to a depth of 25mm (1in). Fill in this area with leaves of thyme. From the base build up the gypsophila, starting with the larger flower heads, and retaining some of the stems.

Continue up the bookmark with the gypsophila, gradually increasing the space between the flowers. Stop just under the crease line. Now add smaller gypsophila, taking care not to fill in too much, or the airy effect will be lost. Cut a piece of protective film larger than the book mark, and carefully rub down from the base making sure not to trap any air bubbles. Trim the film flush.

ANTIQUE MINIATURE

ROMAN FRIEZE

This design is reminiscent of early recorded flower patterns carved in Roman friezes. Choose a landscape-shaped frame about 350mm (14in) wide. Lay the picture back on a bench and cover it with thin wadding. Cut a piece of cream silk to fit the frame, and place on top. Make a soft diamond shape in carrot leaves and add small sprays of lady's mantle, using them to break up the hard outline.

Use green hydrangea florets around the outline and intersperse with small peach coloured potentillas, bringing them in towards the centre. Use larger potentillas further into the centre, tucking in extra foliage to give depth.

Pink potentillas, highlighted against dark foliage and framed in an old gold frame, conjure up thoughts of a Victorian rose garden. Small, old frames can be found in bric-a-brac shops, and are easy to repair and paint. Cut a cream coloured rough surfaced parchment paper to fit the frame, and secure an irregular oval of red-tinged meadowsweet leaves. Place the largest pink potentilla centrally.

Now tuck in large heads of cream candytuft to create lightness. Finally, scatter green florets of guelder rose (cranberry bush) to relieve any solidness. Place the glass and frame over the design/wadding/back 'sandwich'. Slip your fingers underneath with your thumbs on top of the frame. Applying pressure to the sandwich, carefully turn the whole thing over and secure the back.

Fix a further six or seven mixed size potentillas with the largest at the top, interspersing them amongst the foliage to give visual depth. Make the central flower prominent by adding a few leaves under the petals. Finish by adding florets of cow parsnip to create highlights. Place the cleaned glass over the design, turn it over and put it into the frame. Put in some wadding and secure the picture back.

This type of compact posy has retained its popularity for the past century and would fit into any Victorian setting. Cut a piece of imitation parchment paper to fit a circular frame, and lightly pencil on it a 140mm (5½in) diameter circle. Fix tips of carrot leaves around and overlapping the circle. Now add spiraea buds and hedge parsley florets to fill out the circle.

Next take light peach coloured rose petals and fix them around and over the base of the leaves. Turn the paper in an anti-clockwise direction as each petal is secured, overlapping its neighbour, to ensure that you keep a good shape. Now secure a second row of petals over the first.

Take some variegated dogwood leaves and secure them in a circle, positioning the tips half way from the top of the second row of petals. Keep moving the card round in an anti-clockwise direction as you fix the leaves. Now fix a circle of pale blue lobelia over the dogwood.

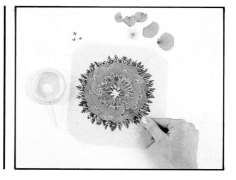

Fix a circle of open spiraea flowers between the first and second row of rose petals, and forget-me-not and hedge parsley florets below the second row of petals. Finally, fix a ring of small rose petals within the lobelia circle and secure a cream potentilla in the centre. Cut a circular mount to fit the frame, allowing space at the perimeter of the design. Frame as usual.

Ｔhe white and blue flowers against a dark background suggests the dawning of a new day. Select a round frame and cut a circle of blue-green paper to fit inside. Secure variegated dogwood leaves in a full crescent, with larger leaves towards the base of the crescent and smaller ones at the tips.

Place a large delphinium at the centre of the crescent. Now use lady's mantle sprays and white melilot spikes to break up the outline. Buds of feverfew and small white potentillas are added towards the ends of the crescent.

Ｃapture the beauty of that special rose. This design needs a round frame about 150mm (6in) in diameter. Cut a mount from coloured paper, then cut a white card to fit the frame. Lay the mount over the white card and very lightly pencil in the inside diameter of the mount. Take single rose leaves and fix each — slightly overlapping — with the leaf tips about 3mm ($\frac{1}{8}$in) from the pencilled circle.

Select large rose petals and repeat the process, with the top of the petals overlapping the leaves by 6mm ($\frac{1}{4}$in). Both the leaves and petals need to be fixed with very small dabs of latex adhesive. When the glue has dried, carefully rub out the pencil line and blow away the rubbings.

Tuck in small buds of delphinium to follow round the shape. Now use large white potentillas and small delphiniums to make an interesting strong centre, and finish the shape with a few further sprays of lady's mantle. Frame in the usual manner with light wadding or plastic foam sheeting under the frame back to provide the necessary pressure to keep the picture in place.

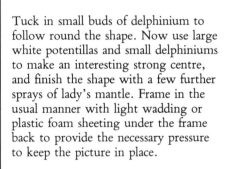

Now form an inner circle with smaller petals in the same way. Select the centre part of a rock rose, put a small dot of adhesive right in the middle of the rose ring, and using a palette knife, slide the rock rose centre in position. Finally, place the mount over the design card, being careful to centre it, and position the cleaned glass over both. Transfer them to the frame and secure the back.

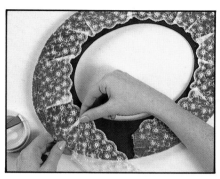

Overtones of lace and a combination of creeping vines and burgundy flowers give a Victorian flavour to this delightful design. Use an oval frame 400mm (16in) across with a burgundy mount, cut slighty wider than your chosen lace. Gather the lace around the mount, folding it at the inside edge and glueing it to the outside edge of the mount.

Cut an oval of 12mm (½in) cellulose wadding to fit exactly the centre of the mount aperture. Place the picture back face up on your bench and put the wadding in the centre. Cover this with oyster coloured silk, trimmed slightly smaller than the frame. Lay autumn leaves to form a crescent and add trails of Russian (silver lace) vine and fuchsia buds to break up the outline.

Add cream potentillas, fools' parsley, buds of cherry blossom and frost-tinged hydrangeas. Create a slightly solid design to give the Victorian look, then lighten the effect with the laced mount, carefully positioning the latter over the design. Next place the cleaned glass over the mount, then finish off the 'sandwich' by adding the picture frame.

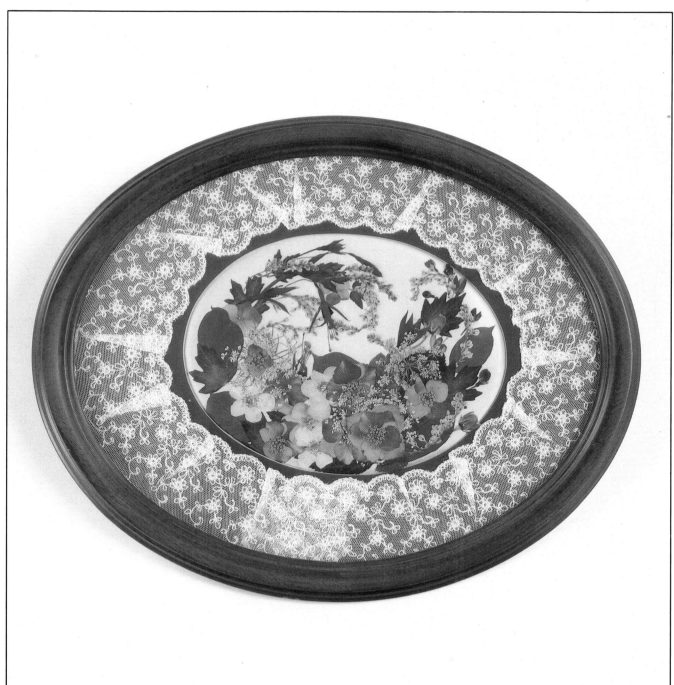

GOLDEN SUMMER

COUNTRY WALK

Memories of a country walk will float back when you view the mixture of grasses and leaves you have gathered and prettily arranged on a sky blue background, framed in natural wood. Fresh young grass stalks, seedheads and small leaves are most suitable; make a 'growing point' using reed canary grass, rice (cord) grass, cocksfoot (orchard) grass and quaking grass.

Having fixed the grasses down with latex adhesive, cut off the excess stems to leave a clear space in the centre. Now fill this in with more grasses, trimming as you go. Finish at the bottom centre with a few knapweed buds and vetch foliage, to give the impression of a 'growing point'. The design is framed without a mount to give a feeling of space.

This frame, reminiscent of garden furniture, and the colourful design suggest bright summer days sitting in the garden. Select cream and brown marbled paper for the background. Fix bracken fern, polypody fern and salad burnet to make an irregular fan shape, taking care to make it asymmetrical.

Use meadowsweet and yellow melilot sprays to fill in between the foliage. Now, using sprays and buds of montbretia, introduce some colour to the left of the design and put a bold spray in the bottom right corner. Create the focal point with a yellow potentilla flower nestled in amongst a large spray of hedge parsley.

Harmonize the whole arrangement by filling in with single flowers of montbretia. Now add further potentilla flowers using a palette knife to help tuck some of the petals under the hedge parsley spray. Place the cleaned glass over the completed design, turn it over and place face down in the picture frame. Add the wadding and picture back and seal it well.

The new 'two pack' varnish makes it possible to seal flowers to many surfaces without altering their form or colour. Once you have mixed the varnish, you will have about two hours to complete each stage. From an art shop buy a sheet of polystyrene foam sandwiched between two lightweight sheets of drawing board. Cut a piece 230mm by 550mm (9in by 20in) with a ruler and craft knife.

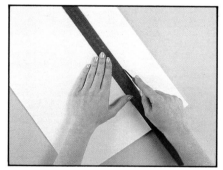

Paint on the board a pale coloured sky and field with water colour paints, and stipple them to achieve a soft effect. Set aside to dry completely.

When the background is dry, mix together a little of the two pack varnish, and apply a coat to the top two thirds of the board. Using a palette knife, start placing various grasses at intervals along the middle section of the board. The varnish will hold them in place. Use a good selection: rye grass, bearded twitch grass, brome grass, meadow fescue and squirrel tailed fescue.

Continue to build up the meadow with crested dog's tail grass, quaking grass, rough meadow grass, tufted hair grass, loose silky bent grass, hare's tail grass and some fennel florets. On the right hand side add yarrow leaves, polypody fern, camomile leaves and spiraea buds to give the impression of distant trees.

Paint a thin line of varnish along the bottom 12mm (½in) and cover this with small dark green leaves to make a solid base. Re-varnish the bottom left half and fill in with more grasses, now adding common knotgrass, knapweed, shepherd's purse, speedwell, periwinkle, daisies, buttercups, lady's bedstraw, wild carrot (Queen Ann's lace), melilot and vetch. Now re-varnish the bottom right half.

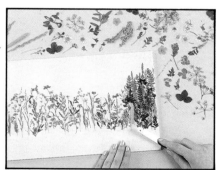

Apply these same plants to the bottom right side. Finally, give two thin coats of varnish (allowing the first to be quite dry before applying the second) to the whole picture area. This delightful scene requires no frame, so simply fix a small ring to the back and hang it on the wall for all to admire.

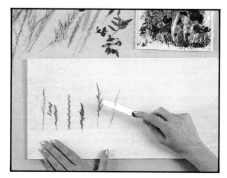

Here's a charming way to provide the bride with an everlasting memento of her wedding day. And there should be plenty of flowers left over to make gifts for other special guests as well, including yourself! See opposite for the bride's picture and on the following pages for guidelines to making the other designs: 57, 65, 66, 73, 77 and 78.

Continue to add more flowers and leaves. If you are using polyanthus, you will find the flowers appear very thin after pressing, so place one on top of another to give greater depth. Using some coloured ribbons saved from the bouquet, stick three short lengths together, and add two loops to form a bow. Fix this in position on one side of the bouquet and add a short length to the other side.

Make up some rosebuds as before and use these to fill in the centre of the design along with some foliage and other flowers; used here are polyanthus, carnation and gypsophila (baby's breath).

If you intend to press the bouquet, ensure the florist does not spray the flowers. Seal the bouquet as soon as possible in a dry plastic box on a bed of tissue paper and keep it in a cool place until you are ready to press it — preferably the next day. Dismantle the bouquet by carefully unwiring each item then press the flowers as described on page 54, leaving under pressure for six weeks.

Make a large open rose by arranging a ring of small overlapping petals on top of a large base petal. Fix sepals to the back of the rose so that they extend beyond the petals and bed the flower in the centre of the design. When complete, frame the picture as usual. The remaining flowers, together with the bridesmaids' bouquets, can be used to make gifts for other members of the wedding party.

Mask a photograph of the bouquet to match the shape of your chosen frame — this will help you to follow the bouquet's design more easily. Lay the picture backing on your work surface and cover it with paper, wadding and ivory silk, cut to size. Using latex adhesive to fix the flowers, copy the shower trail. Make the rosebuds from a few small petals and a couple of sepals.

Now build up the outline with the foliage, moulding the shape to fit comfortably into the frame. Using the photograph as reference, add flowers and buds to the design. Form carnation buds with a few sepals to several petals.

This beautiful ruby satin bow makes a perfect setting for specimen pressings. Take 2½m (2¾yd) of 75mm (3in) wide ribbon, and cut it into three lengths: 500mm (20in), 580mm (23in), and 1.42m (56in). Fold the shortest length, ends to centre, to form a bow and gather the centre using needle and thread. Do the same with the next longest length.

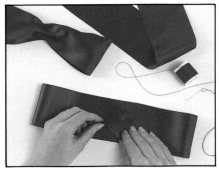

Place the smaller bow on top of the larger one, gather them tightly at the centre, and stitch together. Fold the longest length approximately in half around the centre of the double bow, and sew together at the back to form the knot of the finished bow. Also sew in a small curtain ring at the back by which to hang the design. Trim the ends of the ribbon as shown.

Cut three ovals from beige cartridge paper to fit some miniature plaques. Using a fine pen, write the botanical names of your specimens neatly at the bottom of the ovals. For the first oval, arrange stems, foliage and flowers of forget-me-not to simulate a growing plant. When satisfied with their positioning, fix down with latex adhesive and re-assemble the plaque.

For the second oval, take a large heart's ease (Johnny-jump-up) and fix it one third of the way up from the base, then add further flowers finishing with the smallest at the top. Now introduce heart's ease leaves to give the appearance of a vigorous young plant. When satisfied, fix in position and then carefully assemble within the plaque.

Place a curved stem in the centre of the third oval and fix borage flowers and buds along the stem in a natural way so that it resembles the top of a growing stem. As before, when you have completed the picture, assemble the plaque. Take the three plaques, and arrange them down the ribbon at regular intervals. Now sew them in place, parting the ribbons slightly.

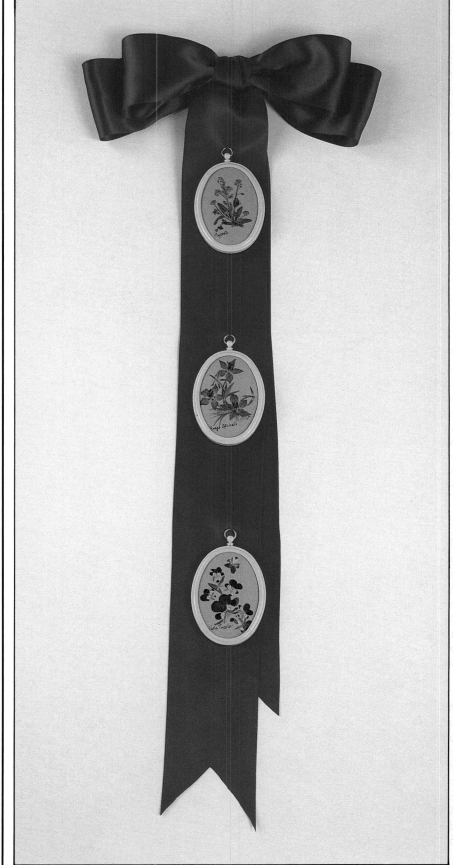

These double peonies should be picked when just open. Strip off the petals and bracts and press between layers of blotting paper, tightening the press daily. After five days change the paper, then tighten the press every three days until ready. Cut some heavy watercolour paper to 520mm by 215mm (20½in by 8½in) and arrange peony leaves in two groups as shown.

Next, fix bamboo leaf sprays, starting at one corner and curving them down towards the opposite corner. Intersperse some sprays between the peony leaf groups.

Away from the picture area, assemble the peony buds. Fix a bract on top of a small petal for the top bud, and another bract on top of two or three petals for the second bud. For the largest bud, use two bracts over four petals. Pick up the buds with tweezers and fix them in position with adhesive, tucking them under the bamboo leaves.

Create the smaller of the two open flowers in position over the ring of peony leaves as follows: using medium sized peony petals, form a ring of overlapping petals around the base of the leaves. Now add a second ring of smaller petals inside the first, and complete the flower by adding wild carrot (Queen Ann's lace) florets to the centre.

Add a few more bamboo leaves to the large ring of peony leaves, and then use some large petals for making the irregular outer circle of the second flower. Fill in with smaller petals to make the second and third circles, and create a centre with wild carrot florets. When complete, make certain that all debris is brushed from the paper before framing the picture.

The clever use of smoke bush (smoketree) on green velvet helps to create a soft misty effect in this striking picture. Remove the back from a rustic frame and cover with wadding and dark green velvet. Start the design by fixing sprays of young ash tree leaves in the shape shown.

Add brown beech leaves and small buds of black knapweed to fill in the outline and create a 'bagpipe' shape.

Suggestions of the 'pipes' are represented by seed heads of pendulous sedge and bottle sedge. Add some spikes of heather to create a solid mass in the centre.

Finally soften the outline by adding the wispy flowers of smoke bush around the edges of the 'bagpipe'. When the design is complete, take care to remove all the dust and pollen from the velvet before placing the cleaned picture glass and frame over it. Slide the frame to the edge of the table and, gripping it firmly, turn it over. Apply pressure to the back of the frame, tack on and seal.

This design's 'just picked' look hides the meticulous care that is needed to make the arrangement. Use cream coloured silk for the background and a good mixture of foliage and grasses for the outline. Secure short stems at the base to represent the flower stalks. Add mixed flowers over the foliage, starting at the top with the palest colours.

Carry on down the sides of the design and then place a head of sweet cicely in the centre to cover the tops of the stems (see above). Start adding the stronger coloured flowers, fixing a large yellow *Kerria* over the sweet cicely. Finally, soften the outline by adding flowers that droop down to the base of the bunch (see below). Choose a rustic frame, pad this out and closely seal the back.

The colours and fine grain of this beautiful cherrywood box are complemented by the subtle arrangement of autumnal foliage. Begin by creating and 'L' shaped outline with leaves of Japanese maple, autumn cherry, willow, wayfaring tree, hawthorn, sumach and smoke bush (smoketree).

Continue adding the foliage, using sufficient adhesive to fix each leaf securely. Trim any overlapping pieces, so as to avoid excess bulkiness. When you are happy with the shape, coat it with a thin layer of matt varnish.

Now add small buds of blue lobelia, creating a sweeping curve throughout the outline. Use larger, open flowers in a cluster at the left and base of the design to form the focal point. Finish with two thin coats of varnish.

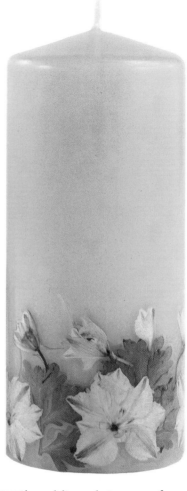

T his is a simple but elegant way to use empty gift boxes as containers or pot-pourri. We have selected a reen and a black box. Take the lid off ne of the boxes and lightly secure hree whole flower heads of cow arsley diagonally across it. With erosol spray paint, give the top of the ox two light coats of gold paint.

When the paint is dry, remove the parsley to reveal the unsprayed part of the box. This shows up as a pretty pattern through the paint. Now fix the gold sprayed cow parsley to the other box lid. These boxes are filled with 'Noel' pot-pourri, which is a festive mixture of small cones, tree bark and citrus peel. Cover the pot-pourri with cling film (plastic wrap) before replacing the lids.

T hese delicate designs transform ordinary thick candles. But be very careful not to let the candle burn down below the protective film, as the designs are not flameproof! For the yellow candle fix three autumn sumach leaves in a spray with latex adhesive. Repeat twice around the candle.

The other candle is offset with five pink larkspur flowers fixed around the base. Rue leaves are tucked in and around the flowers. Finally, add some larkspur buds a little above the foliage. Carefully cover the designs on both candles with protective film, allowing an extra 5mm (¼in) above the design. Rub the film down carefully and avoid trapping any air bubbles.

The dramatic effect of white flowers against a black silk background enhances the silver plated trinket box to create a sophisticated gift. These trinket boxes can be readily purchased from craft shops. Open up the lid assembly and take out the foam padding. Cut a circle of black silk to cover the padding.

Secure sprays of miniature variegated rose leaves in a crescent shape. Now add sprays and single flowers of gypsophila (baby's breath), tucking the stems under the leaves where necessary.

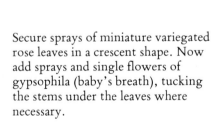

Starting at the tips of the crescent, and building to the centre, add buds and flowers of feverfew. Place a large full flower of feverfew towards the bottom centre to create a focal point. When the design is complete, cover it with the plastic sheet from the lid, and assemble according to the manufacturer's instructions.

This heart shaped trinket box makes a pretty gift for someone you love. Cut a heart shaped piece of ivory silk to fit the lid. Now cut 75mm (3in) of 6mm (¼in) wide ivory satin ribbon. Fold the ribbon in half, trim each end and glue to a small geranium leaf. Fix this near the point of the heart as shown.

Fix another leaf on top of the fold in the ribbon and then add leaves alternatively to the right and the left, building up a heart shaped outline. When the shape is complete, fix florets of cow parsley over the inner edge of the leaves.

Fill the centre of the heart with rich red verbena. Finally, fix a small ivory satin bow to the top of the heart as shown below and assemble the box lid according to the manufacturer's instructions.

Once you have gained confidence in using larger flowers, you will find this miniature design an exciting challenge. Buy a miniature crystal bowl (available from good craft shops) and use the white card from its lid as the design card. Start by fixing the tiny foliage of shepherd's purse in place to make a full crescent outline.

Fill in the outline with florets of yellow and pink alyssum and elderberry flowers. To fix the flowers in position first place a tiny spot of latex adhesive in the required place and, using a paint brush, gently tease a flower over it, then press it to secure.

Finally, tuck in heart's ease (Johnny-jump-up), keeping the largest to make a focal point towards the bottom centre of the design. Place the plastic circle from the lid over the finished design, and assemble according to the maker's instructions.

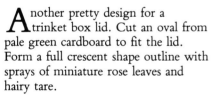

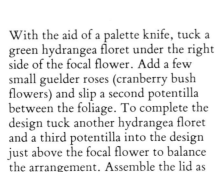

Another pretty design for a trinket box lid. Cut an oval from pale green cardboard to fit the lid. Form a full crescent shape outline with sprays of miniature rose leaves and hairy tare.

Now follow the outline with tendrils and buds of vetch. For the focal point, choose an open peach potentilla and fix it to the base of the crescent, slightly off centre.

With the aid of a palette knife, tuck a green hydrangea floret under the right side of the focal flower. Add a few small guelder roses (cranberry bush flowers) and slip a second potentilla between the foliage. To complete the design tuck another hydrangea floret and a third potentilla into the design just above the focal flower to balance the arrangement. Assemble the lid as instructed.

Paperweights, specially designed to hold craftwork, are readily available from craft suppliers. In this design, a stunning arrangement for that special birthday is easily created with a few flowers. Begin by cutting a black card to fit the oval recess of the paperweight. Paint the figure '21' in white to the right of the oval.

Break up mugwort foliage and, keeping the white underside uppermost, fit it to the card following the outline of the oval. Where the foliage meets the '21', add some budded sprays of gypsophila (baby's breath).

Intersperse a few open flowers of gypsophila amongst the foliage then create the focal point with a large open flower of white larkspur. To complete the design, tuck a small larkspur flower under the leaves above the focal point, and place a larkspur bud below. Position the design card inside the recess of the paperweight, pad out with foam if necessary, and seal with the self-adhesive baize.

If you don't feel up to scripting the words for this attractive paperweight design, see if you can locate a caligrapher or illustrator to do it for you. Cut the paper on which the words are inscribed to fit into the paperweight's recess. Surround your quotation or verse with several sprigs of thyme foliage.

Intersperse the foliage with a pretty range of minute flowers: shown here are spiraea, forget-me-not, red alyssum, star of Bethlehem, buds of Japanese crab apple, thyme and melilot. To fix each flower, put a dot of latex adhesive in the required place on the design card and tease the flower into position with a paintbrush; press lightly to secure.

To complete the design add a few buds and flowers of the hebe 'Simon Delux' and some yellow alyssum. Finally, place a heart's ease (Johnny-jump-up) to the right of the verse before fitting the design into the paperweight and sealing it with the self-adhesive baize supplied.

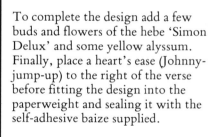

Not every arrangement need be pretty and feminine. This design is perfect for any man's desk. Cut a piece of cardboard to fit the recess of the paperweight and place a thin layer of latex adhesive along one edge. Fix to the strip of adhesive a selection of leaves, overlapping each other and the edge. Repeat for the other three sides then trim the leaves flush with the side of the cardboard.

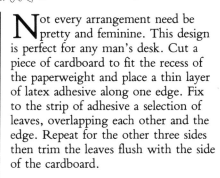

Fill in the centre of the design with smaller leaves. Shown here are hawthorn, virginia creeper, flowering cherry, spiraea, *Euonymus,* smoke bush (smoketree), and *Acaena* 'Copper Carpet'. Overlap the foliage randomly to create a more natural appearance.

When the design is complete, fit it into the recess of the paperweight. If necessary, pad out with foam before sealing with the self-adhesive baize supplied.

Commemorate a special event with this highly individual paper-weight. Cut a circle of white cardboard to fit inside the recess of the paperweight. Divide the circle into eight equal segments using a fine pencil, then draw a 25mm (1in) gold circle in the centre. Outline the circle inside and out with a black pen and mark out the segments with gold.

Inside the centre circle write the date that you wish to commemorate with a black pen. Now form a background on each segment with small sprays of yarrow foliage. Secure them with the stems toward the centre.

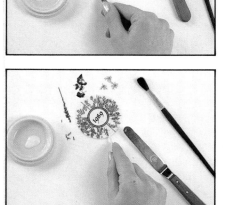

On two opposite segments place several buds of pale pink candytuft and an open flower at the centre. In the opposing segments use single flowers of yellow melilot, red alyssum and segments of sweet cicely. Put the design inside the paperweight recess and pad out with foam if necessary. Seal the design with the self-adhesive baize supplied.

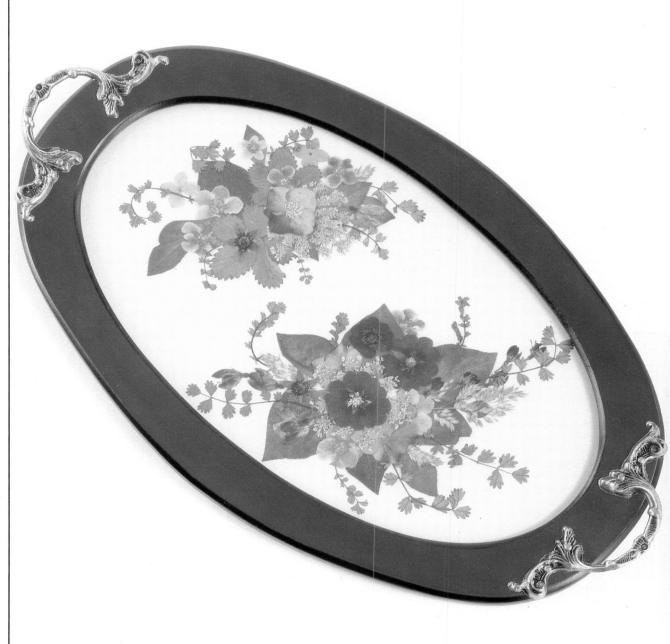

Afternoon tea takes on real elegance with this striking tray purchased from craft suppliers. Fix a cluster of autumn plumbago leaves at one end of the oval card (supplied with the tray) and at the other end fix a smaller cluster of plumbago and autumn wild strawberry leaves. Now enlarge and fill out these two clusters with leaf sprays of *Acaena* 'Blue Haze'. Keep each cluster fairly oval in shape.

Working first on the smaller cluster, create a focal point with a red-tinged green hydrangea flower sitting on top of a wild carrot (Queen Ann's lace) flowerhead. Now form a gentle curve of pink potentilla across the top of the cluster and finish off with green hydrangea and red saxifrage. For the focal point of the larger cluster place a deep red potentilla on top of a head of wild carrot.

To add depth, tuck some pink potentilla and red-tinged hydrangea under the carrot head. Now place two smaller 'Red Ace' potentillas above the focal point. Make a gentle diagonal curve into the centre of the design with buds of Japanese crab apple and finish off with sprays of greyhair grass. Reassemble the tray according to the manufacturer's instructions.

FUCHSIA PLACE MAT

CARNATION COASTERS

An ingenious idea which adds individuality to any table setting. Begin by cutting a rectangle of hardboard 215mm by 280mm (8½in by 11in). Round off the corners with sandpaper. Next, cut a piece of green marbled paper to fit the hardboard. Draw two double-lined borders with green pen in opposite corners, as shown.

Using foliage of the *Ranunculus* 'Bachelor's Buttons', make a triangular shape in the top left corner and an 'L' shape in the bottom right. Add fuchsias to the triangle, beginning with a bud at the apex, gradually adding more open flowers and finishing at the widest part with a full flower. Repeat the process on the 'L' shape, using fuchsia buds at the tips and a full flower in the centre.

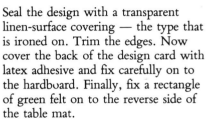
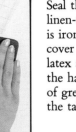

Seal the design with a transparent linen-surface covering — the type that is ironed on. Trim the edges. Now cover the back of the design card with latex adhesive and fix carefully on to the hardboard. Finally, fix a rectangle of green felt on to the reverse side of the table mat.

These glass drinks coasters — readily available from craft shops — lend themselves to a carnation display. Cut a circle of moss green paper to fit into the recess of the large bottle coaster. Now fix large petals of yellow carnation, overlapping them slightly, to form an outer circle.

Fill in the outer circle with smaller carnation petals to create a second circle. Small petals from the centre of the carnation make up the final inner circle. To complete the display fix cow parsley florets to the centre.

Fit the design card into the recess of the bottle coaster and seal with the circle of baize supplied. Repeat this process for each drinks coaster, using different colours for an attractive display.

The combination of cream coloured blossom and lace prettily complement traditional china at the dinner table. Cut a rectangle of dark brown cardboard 110mm by 80mm (4½in by 3¼in). Crease and fold it widthways to form a 'tent'. Using a gold marker pen carefully write the desired name in the centre of the top page.

Take about 300mm (12in) of cream lace and, starting about three quarters of the way along the folded edge, fix it to the card with a little latex adhesive. Pinch the lace to form gathers as you round the corners and fix with a little extra adhesive.

Select a colour to complement the bride's attendants and these place cards will enhance the wedding feast. Cut a rectangle of cardboard 170mm by 65mm (6½in by 2½in); crease and fold it widthways. Select some grained silver paper and, using a template, mark and cut out an oval 37mm by 55mm (1½in by 2¼in). Trim the silver paper to 55mm by 75mm (2¼in by 3in), keeping the oval centred.

Glue the silver paper cut-out centrally to the front of the card using a glue pen. With latex adhesive, fix some carrot leaves in a crescent shape at the top right corner, and slightly smaller ones to the bottom left. Place a small head of fools' parsley centrally on each crescent.

Using the buds and open flowers of blackthorn, make an 'L' shape at the top right corner. Use an open flower to cover the join in the lace. Create the focal point by using a pair of open flowers, glued one on top of the other. This will also give these delicate flowers greater depth. Make a similar shape, but without the focal point, at the bottom left corner.

Build up on these corner designs with pink candytuft florets and more pieces of fools' parsley to give an elegant balance.

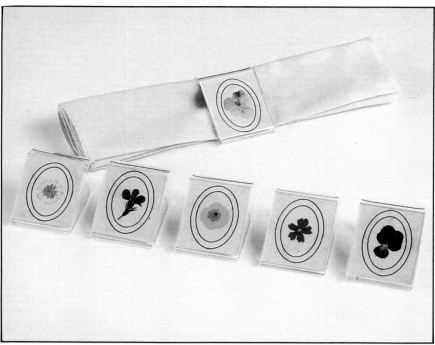

This napkin holder offers a delightful alternative to the standard napkin ring. Cut 1½m (5ft) of 40mm (1½in) wide peach satin ribbon. About 100mm (4in) from one end fix a peach potentilla. Tuck melilot foliage above and below this, then add three spikes of white melilot above. Arrange an identical display about 50mm (2in) from the other end of the ribbon.

Cut two strips of protective film, about 200mm (8in) long, and cover the ends of the ribbon. Firmly stroke out any air bubbles. Trim the ends of the ribbon into 'V' shapes. Finally, tie the ribbon into a generous bow around a triangular napkin arrangement, allowing one end to fall slightly longer than the other, as shown.

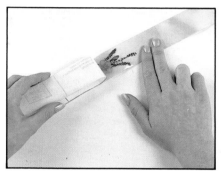

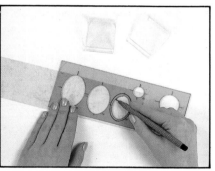

These simple but attractive napkin rings can be purchased from craft suppliers and make a perfect complement to any dinner party. On a strip of green marbled cardboard, mark out an oval 50mm by 37mm (2in by 1¼in) with a green pen. Inside this oval, mark out a smaller one, also in green. You will need a template to achieve an accurate shape.

Repeat this procedure using a wide range of different coloured flowers; used here are buttercup, blue lobelia, daisy, red verbena and different varieties of pansy.

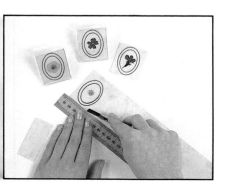

In the centre of the ovals, fix an attractive flowerhead. Cover the design with protective film, smoothing out any air bubbles. With the aid of a steel rule and craft knife, trim the strip to fit the napkin holder.

Russian vine (silver lace vine) is a natural creeper, so it is in an ideal setting, creeping and climbing over this pine coat rack. First, sand the wood thoroughly before applying one coat of 'two pack' varnish.

With the aid of a palette knife, start to adhere sprays of Russian vine to the varnish, putting them at various heights along the length of the rack. Add a few leaves and single sprays to fill in.

Cover the vine stem ends as you go with the feathery foliage of camomile. When the design is complete, and the varnish dry, apply two further coats of varnish.

Feverfew flowers and rose leaves transform a simple letter rack into a handsome writing table accessory. Start by coating the front face of the bottom rack with matt varnish. Place a spray of rose leaves on the left hand side, pointing upwards from the bottom corner. Add a feverfew bud just above the first leaf and a flower at the end of the spray.

Position a second rose leaf spray next to the first, this time pointing it downwards. Continue in this way across the rack, adding feverfew flowers between the sprays. When the design is dry, give two further coats of thin varnish. Follow the whole procedure once again for the top rack.

O nce again, a plain wooden container is enhanced by the addition of a few flowers. Begin by varnishing the front of the utensil holder. With a palette knife gently ease into position an oval outline of feverfew foliage.

P lain pine book ends can easily be decorated using a selection of pressed flowers. Begin by painting one book end with matt varnish. While the varnish is still sticky, create a loose triangular shape, starting with a miniature rose leaf spray and buds of blue delphinium.

Starting at the top of the outline, fill in with buds of feverfew, gradually working down the design with both buds and flowers. Finish at the base of the foliage with the largest feverfew flowers to create a focal point. Tuck in extra leaves to fill any gaps and when the design is dry, finish with four further coats of varnish.

Working in gentle curves, position peach potentillas to the left and delphiniums to the right of the design. Scatter spiraea 'Snowball' florets throughout, and finish by extending the outline with a few small leaves. When dry, coat the design again with two thin coats of matt varnish.

These specially designed door plates, available from craft suppliers, can be decorated to suit the decor of any room. Cut a piece of protective film to cover the back of the plate and a piece of foam to fit the centre of the plate without overlapping the holes. Then cut a rectangle of coloured cardboard to fit the recess and punch holes in the corners to match those in the plate.

Create the design above with the narcissus 'Sol d'Or' and tiny florets of cornflower. Place the design card in the recess at the back of the plate, pad out with the foam and seal the back with protective film. The design below is made with sprays of montbretia buds, autumn leaves and potentilla. The third example contains specimens of meadowsweet, buttercup and cowslip.

Now return to the top rung. Place three rose leaves in the centre of the garland, and add a small spray of cow parsley and florets of red alyssum to the tip of each leaf.

Position a single larkspur bud at either end of the garland. Now take two medium sized larkspur flowers and place them equidistant from the centre, at the high points of the garland. Finish with a large pink larkspur in the centre. The completed design is shown below on a larger scale to help you see more detail.

When both rungs have dried completely, apply two or three coats of varnish to seal the designs. Be quite sure that each coat is dry before applying the next.

Thís pretty chalet-style chair is child size, but you can just as easily create the design shown here on a full scale chair. Lay the chair down on to your work surface and coat the front of the top rung with 'two pack' varnish. Now form a wavy garland using the trailing stems of 'mind-your-own-business' plant, leaving a gap in the middle. In between the leaves place single florets of red alyssum.

When dry, apply another thin coat of varnish in preparation for the next flowers. Now varnish the lower rung. Place a large red alyssum in the centre and add a short trail of mind-your-own-business to the left. At the end of this trail add another, smaller head of alyssum, before finishing with just a few mind-your-own-business leaves. This forms half the garland. Repeat on the right side.

Blue lobelia is an attractive addition to plain yellow enamel. Start by marking out a rectangular area on the side of the pot with masking tape. Now lay the pot on its side, securing it to your work surface with an adhesive putty such as Blu-Tack. Paint the area with a thin coat of 'two pack' varnish. Take care the varnish does not build up at the tape edge and form a ridge.

While the first coat of varnish is still sticky, position several carrot leaves to form a teardrop shape outline. When this design is completely dry, add another coat of varnish.

Now, fill in with the flowers. Use lobelia, beginning with buds at the top and coming down to the base with larger flowers. Fill in any gaps with foliage and add a couple of budded stems at the base to create a natural effect. When this is dry, remove the tape and give a final coat of varnish, feathering the edges by wiping them with a lint-free cloth.

This type of white enamel canister can be bought either new or second hand. Secure the canister to your work surface with blobs of adhesive putty. Now take a large head of mauve candytuft and fit to the centre of the canister with latex adhesive. Surround the flower with salad burnet leaves and add two more candytuft flowers on either side. Paint over the design with 'two pack' varnish.

For the canister lid, coat with varnish before positioning a circle of salad burnet leaves — slightly apart — around the knob. Fill in between the leaves with large, single candytuft flowers. When dry, seal this design with two thin coats of varnish, feathering the edges with a lint-free cloth.

Transform a 'sample' coffee jar into a pretty herb or spice container. If you have several of these jars, you can make a whole series. Apply a thin coat of 'two pack' varnish to the front of the jar and position some carrot foliage and gypsophila (baby's breath) to form the outline.

Complete the floral design with some grass and a verbena flower. When the first coat of varnish is dry, apply a second coat, over the design, feathering the edges of the varnish with a lint-free cloth.

Cut a circle from white sticky-back plastic to fit the top of the lid. Repeat the floral design on the plastic, fixing the plants with latex adhesive. Cover the design with protective film and fix the circle to the lid. For that finishing touch, add a band of broderie anglaise around the lid.

This solid perfume is simple to make, and looks so pretty in a matching green ceramic jar: a perfect complement to any dressing table. Begin creating the floral design on the insert card supplied with the lid. Fix three variegated geranium leaves in a triangular shape using latex adhesive.

Follow this outline with silverweed, yellow medick and two wood avens (clove root) flowers. Complete with a large wood avens flower at the base. Reassemble the lid.

To make the perfume you will need 3 tsp of shredded beeswax, 2 tsp of almond oil, 15 drops of your chosen concentrated perfume oil and a drop of sap-green dye. Slowly melt the wax and almond oil over a very low heat. Remove the pan from the heat and, when the mixture has cooled a little, add the perfume and colour and pour it into the trinket box. It will then set hard and be ready for use.

A gold pendant makes a delightful setting for a delicate cream and brown design. Cut an oval of brown cardboard to fit, then select small cream buds and flowers of traveller's joy and hawthorn, and sprays of autumn coloured *Acaena microphylla* leaves. Form a soft crescent of leaves, placing dots of adhesive directly on to the card and teasing each leaf into place with a paintbrush.

Now add buds of traveller's joy and sprays of *Acaena* to complete the full crescent shape, using a toothpick to place the adhesive directly on to the back of the larger flowers.

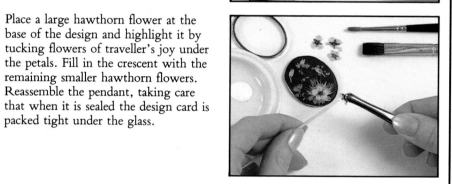

Place a large hawthorn flower at the base of the design and highlight it by tucking flowers of traveller's joy under the petals. Fill in the crescent with the remaining smaller hawthorn flowers. Reassemble the pendant, taking care that when it is sealed the design card is packed tight under the glass.

This exquisite piece of matching jewellery simply needs a little patience to complete. Cut a white cardboard oval to fit the brooch and fix sprays of miniature maidenhair fern to create an outline. Scatter gypsophila (baby's breath) buds amongst the foliage, then add a cluster of red alyssum in the centre and a few blue forget-me-nots.

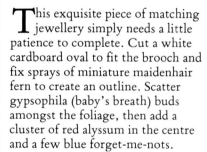

Now cut a white oval to fit the pendant. With the aid of toothpicks, fix two sprays of shepherd's purse foliage to the top and right of the card. Arrange flower stems to resemble the stems of a bunch of flowers. Now add curving gypsophila buds throughout the design.

Add buds of spiraea and shepherd's purse next, teasing them into place, over dots of adhesive, with a soft paintbrush. Use an open flower of red alyssum to form the focal point and bring some spiraea through the design from the left to the centre. Assemble the jewellery according to the manufacturer's instructions.

MAHOGANY BROOCH

ANTIQUE BROOCH

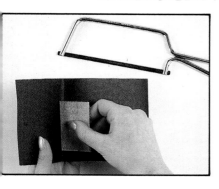

Make this delightful brooch from scratch! With a hacksaw cut a rectangle of thin mahogany 50mm by 75mm (2in by 3in). Round off the corners, front and back, with sandpaper. Give the brooch one thin coat of varnish and when completely dry, sand and varnish it again.

Form an outline on the sticky varnish with leaves of rock geranium, meadowsweet and common bent grass. Across this outline create a curving line of hawthorn flowers, tucking a few more leaves of rock geranium beneath the flowers as you go.

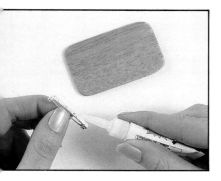

When the design is complete, coat with two or three layers of varnish, allowing each coat to dry in between applications. Finally, attach a brooch pin to the back of the wood with 'super' strong adhesive.

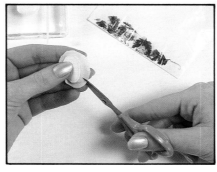

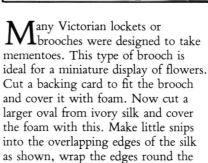

Many Victorian lockets or brooches were designed to take mementoes. This type of brooch is ideal for a miniature display of flowers. Cut a backing card to fit the brooch and cover it with foam. Now cut a larger oval from ivory silk and cover the foam with this. Make little snips into the overlapping edges of the silk as shown, wrap the edges round the backing card and glue down.

With latex adhesive fix a tip of frosted cow parsley leaf in the centre of the oval. At the top add pale peach candytuft and a wisp of common bent grass. Place more grass down the side of the design.

Add peach bistort to the left and red flowers of the spiraea 'Anthony Waterer' to the right and foreground. Finally, place an open flower of candytuft in the centre to form the focal point. Seal the design into the brooch using either the original backing or, if this is missing, packing it into an oval of thick cardboard.

SCIENTIFIC CLASSIFICATION

The following is an alphabetical list of the common names of plants
used in this book and their Latin equivalents.

Common name	Latin name	Common name	Latin name	Common name	Latin name	Common name	Latin name
Acroclinium (sunray)	*Acroclinium roseum = Helipterum roseum*	Euonymus	*Euonymus japonicus*	Lotus	*Nelumbo lutea*	Russian vine (silver lace vine)	*Polygonum aubertii*
Alyssum	*Alyssum*	Fennel	*Foeniculum vulgare*	Love-in-a-mist	*Nigella damascena*		
Apple blossom	*Malus sylvestris*	Feverfew	*Chrysanthemum parthenium*	Love-lies-bleeding	*Amaranthus caudatus*	Rye grass	*Lolium perenne*
Astrantia	*Astrantia*			Maidenhair fern	*Adiantum pedatum*	Salad burnet	*Sanguisorba minor*
Ash	*Fraxinus excelsior*	Flowering currant	*Ribes sanguineum*	Maple	*Acer campestre*	Sandflower (winged everlasting)	*Ammobium alatum*
'Bachelor's Buttons' buttercup	*Ranunculus aconitifolius*	Fools' parsley	*Aethusa cynapium*	Meadow fescue	*Festuca pratensis*		
		Forget-me-not	*Myosotis*	Meadowsweet	*Filipendula ulmaria*	Saxifrage	*Saxifraga moschata*
Bamboo	*Arundinaria*	Fuchsia	*Fuchsia magellanica*	Medick, yellow	*Medicago*	Sea holly	*Eryngium olivierianum*
Barley, black-eared	*Hordeum*	Geranium	*Pelargonium*	Melilot	*Melilotus*	Sea lavender	*Limonium tataricum = Goniolimon tataricum*
Beard grass	*Polypogon*	Glixia (grass daisy)	*Aphyllanthes monspeliensis*	Mind-your-own-business	*Helxine soleirolii*		
Bearded twitch grass	*Agropyrom caninum*	Globe thistle	*Echinops*			Shepherd's purse	*Capella bursa-pastoris*
Beech	*Fagus sylvatica*	Golden rod	*Solidago*	Montbretia	*Crocosmia rocosmiiflora*	Silverweed	*Potentilla anserina*
Bistort	*Polygonum bistorta*	Greyhair grass	*Corynephorus canescens*	Mugwort	*Artemisia vulgaris*	Smoke bush (smoketree)	*Cotinus coggygria*
Blackthorn	*Prunus spinosa*	Guelder rose (cranberry bush)	*Viburnum opulus*	Nipplewort (or broom bloom)	*Laspana communis*		
'Blue Haze'	*Acaena*					Snowdrop	*Galanthus nivalis*
Borage	*Borago officinalis*	Gypsophila (baby's breath)	*Gypsophila paniculata*	Oats, wild	*Avena fatua*	'Sol d'Or'	*Narcissus tazetta*
Bottlebrush	*Callistemon*	Hairy tare vetch	*Vicia hirsuta*	Pansy	*Viola*	Speedwell	*Veronica officinalis*
Bracken fern	*Pteridium aquilinum*	Hare's or rabbit's tail grass	*Lagurus ovatus*	Pearl everlasting	*Anaphalis*	Spiraea (spring flowering)	*Spiraea 'Arguta'*
Brome grass	*Bromus commutatus*			Peony	*Paeonia lactiflora*		
Buttercup	*Ranunculus acris*	Hawthorn	*Crataegus monogyna*	Periwinkle	*Vinca minor*	Spiraea (summer flowering)	*Spiraea bumalda*
Camomile	*Matricaria matricariodes*	Heart's ease (Johnny-jump-up)	*Viola tricolor*	Plumbago	*Plumbago capensis*		
Candytuft	*Iberis umbellata*			Polyanthus	*Primula polyantha*	Squirrel tailed fescue	*Festuca bromides*
Carnation	*Dianthus carophyllus*	Heather	*Erica*	Polypody fern	*Polypodium*	Star of Bethlehem	*Ornithogalum umbellatum*
Carrot foliage	*Daucus carota*	Hebe	*Hebe*	Poppy	*Papaver*		
Cherry blossom	*Prunus sargentii*	Hedge bedstraw	*Galium album*	Potentilla (shrubby)	*Potentilla fruticosa*	Statice	*Limonium sinuatum*
Chervil	*Chaerophyllum temulentum*	Hedge parsley	*Torilis japonica*	Potentilla (woody)	*Potentilla nepalensis*	Strawflower or everlasting	*Helichrysum*
		Honesty (silver dollar plant)	*Lunaria annua*	Primrose	*Primula vulgaris*		
Chinese lantern	*Physalis alkekengi*			Quaking grass	*Briza media* and *Briza maxima*	Sumach	*Rhus typhina*
Clubrush	*Scirpus*	Hop trefoil	*Trifolium campestre*			Sunray	*Helipterum*
Cocksfoot grass (orchard grass)	*Dactylis glomerata*	Horseshoe vetch	*Hippocrepis comosa*	Rat's tail statice	*Limonium suworowii = Psylliostachys suworowii*	Sweet cicely	*Myrrhis odorata*
		Hydrangea	*Hydrangea*			Thyme	*Thymus serpyllum*
Common bent grass	*Agrostis tenuis*	Japanese crab apple	*Malus floribunda*			Traveller's joy	*Clematis vitalba*
'Copper Carpet'	*Acaena*	Japanese maple	*Acer palmatum*	Reed	*Phragmites australis*	Tufted hair grass	*Deschampsia cespitosa*
Cornflower	*Centaurea cyanus*	Knapweed	*Centaurea nigra*	Reed grass (also reed canary grass)	*Phalaris arundinacea*	Verbena	*Verbena hybrida*
Cow parsley	*Anthriscus sylvestris*	Knotgrass	*Polygonum aviculare*			Vetch	*Vicia sativa*
Cow parsnip	*Heracleum sphondylium*	Lady's bedstraw	*Galium verum*	Rhodanthe (sunray or Swan River everlasting)	*Rhodanthe manglesii = Helipterum manglesii*	Virginia creeper	*Parthenocissus quinquefolia*
Cowslip	*Primula veris*	Lady's mantle	*Alchemilla alpina* and *Alchemilla mollis*				
Creeping bent grass	*Agrostis stolonifera*			Rice grass (cordgrass)	*Spartina*	Wayfaring tree	*Viburnum lantana*
Creeping cinquefoil	*Potentilla reptans*	Larkspur	*Delphinium consolida*	Rock geranium	*Geranium cinereum*	Whitebeam	*Sorbus aria*
Crested dog's tail grass	*Cynosurus cristatus*	Lavender	*Lavandula angustifolia = L. spica* or *L. officinalis*	Rock rose	*Cistus*	Wild carrot (Queen Ann's lace)	*Daucus carota*
Daisy	*Bellis perennis*			Rose	*Rosa*		
Delphinium	*Delphinium elatum*			Rose bay willow herb	*Epilobium angustifolium*	Wild strawberry	*Fragaria vesca*
Dogwood	*Cornus alba spaethii*	Lobelia	*Lobelia erinus*	Rough meadow grass	*Poa trivialis*	Willow	*Salix*
Elderberry	*Sambucus nigra*	Loose silky bent grass	*Apera spica-venti*	Rue	*Ruta graveolens*	Wood avens (clove root)	*Geum urbanum*
						Yarrow	*Achillea*

DRYING METHODS

Suitable Plants for Preserving in Desiccants

Anemone	Hellibore
Bells of Ireland	Hollyhock
Buttercup	Larkspur
Camellia	Lily flowerheads
Cornflower	Marigold
Daffodil	Mimosa
Dahlia	Monkshood
Daisy	Orchid
Delphinium	Paeony
Elderberry	Pansy
Forget-me-not	Primrose
Freesia	Ranunculus
Gentian	Rose
Geranium	Violet

Suitable Plants for Preserving in Glycerine

Aspidistra leaves	Ivy leaves
Barley	Lady's mantle
Beech leaves	Laurel leaves
Bells of Ireland	Magnolia leaves
Box leaves	Mahonia leaves
Bracken fern	Oak leaves
Chestnut leaves	Oats
Eucalyptus leaves	Old man's beard
Hawthorn leaves	Quaking grass
Holly leaves	Rabbit's or hare's tail grass
Hops	
Hydrangea	Wheat

Suitable Plants for Air Drying

Acanthus	Eucalyptus leaves	Iris seedheads	Protea
Acroclinium	Gladioli seedheads	Lady's mantle	Rhodanthe
Anaphalis	Globe thistle seedheads	Larkspur	Rose
Bamboo	Golden rod	Lavender	Sea holly
Barley	Grasses	Lotus seedheads	Sea lavender
Bells of Ireland	Gypsophila	Love-in-a-mist	Shepherd's purse
Bottlebrush	Heather	Lupin seedheads	Statice
Chinese lantern	Helichrysum	Mimosa	Sunray
Clary	Hogweed seedheads	Monkshood	Sweetcorn
Cornflower	Hollyhock seedheads	Moss	Teasel seedheads
Cow parsley seedheads	Honesty seedheads	Oats	Thistle seedheads
Delphinium	Hops	Onion seedheads	Wheat
Dock	Hydrangea	Poppy seedheads	Xeranthemum

INDEX

ACKNOWLEDGEMENTS

The publishers would like to thank the following for their
help in compiling this book:

Longmans Ltd. Florist, 46 Holborn Viaduct, London EC1,
(for making the wedding bouquet on page 71).

Framecraft Miniatures Ltd., 148-150 High Street, Aston, Birmingham.

SUPPLIERS

Swan House Gallery, Ashfield, Stowmarket, Suffolk, England.
(Shop and mail order service run by author Mary Lawrence, specialized in the sale of pressed
flower accessories and designs, including presses, mounts, frames and wooden kits plus a
wide range of other items for displaying craftwork).

Mail order suppliers of items designed to display craftwork (such as porcelain
and crystal boxes, plaques, paperweights, fingerplates and napkin rings):

Framecraft Miniatures Ltd., 148-150 High Street, Aston, Birmingham, UK.
(supplying UK and Europe)

Anne Brinkley Designs, 21 Ransom Road, Newton Centre, Mass. 02159, USA.

Needlecraft International Pty. Ltd., 19 Railway Parade, Eastwood, NSW 2122, Australia.

Mrs Greville Parker, 286 Queen Street, Masterton, New Zealand.